What It's Like to Walk With the
Holy Spirit

NORMAN WEBER

ISBN 978-1-64079-877-9 (paperback)
ISBN 978-1-64079-878-6 (digital)

Copyright © 2017 by Norman Weber

All rights reserved. No part of this publication may be reproduced, distributed, or transmitted in any form or by any means, including photocopying, recording, or other electronic or mechanical methods without the prior written permission of the publisher. For permission requests, solicit the publisher via the address below.

Christian Faith Publishing, Inc.
832 Park Avenue
Meadville, PA 16335
www.christianfaithpublishing.com

Printed in the United States of America

Chapter 1

In the Beginning

ACHILLES TENDON REATTACHED

I received a telephone call on a Sunday evening from a pastor I knew who lived seventy-five kilometres away. He was in his early sixties and had slid into home plate playing baseball and tore his Achilles tendon in his ankle. He asked if he could come by the following morning on the way to the hospital to have it operated on. He said, "I want you to pray that it is reattached." I asked the Holy Spirit how to pray, and He said, "Extend your hands out and have him put his ankle into your hands and command the tendon to be reattached in the name of Jesus." I did exactly that the following morning and told him to go to the hospital and they would confirm that it was reattached, and that is exactly what happened. God is good, and when we learn to do exactly as the Holy Spirit shows us, we will see many miracles that our Lord does. I have been encouraged by the Holy Spirit to write this book. I pray that it will be an encouragement to you.

RAISED IN WINDSOR, ONTARIO

I was born and raised in the Windsor, Ontario, area. As a child, I was very shy and quiet. I had few friends. I never volunteered to answer a single question in school, unless I was asked. I had the smarts to do well, though, and I remember in high school, there was a contest between a Jewish fellow and myself, and in grade 10, I had the highest marks in the class. The Jewish fellow went on to become a famous lawyer.

INFLUENCE OF SUNDAY SCHOOL

I was taken to Sunday school in a denominational church and transferred to another church in town as my father knew the pastor. I was confirmed at age 14 and became the head usher. I was required to go to the pastor's office each Sunday before church for instructions; there were very few though. However, this pastor shared a three- to four-minute story with me every Sunday morning for years that had a Christian tone to it. It was like he was sandpapering all the rough spots off me. I didn't realize it at the time, but he had a real influence on me and the forming of my attitude and character.

ACQUIRING THE LIVING BIBLE

Following grade 13, I apprenticed with a chartered accountant firm for five years and passed all the exams and became a CA. A principle was developing in my mind, and that was as I did a good job for the company, I would be awarded with pay raises and promotions. I could size up a company at age 21 or 22 and make recommendations to the clients, and they would not believe me and ask the partner in the firm who would confirm what I had said. I carried this principle forward in my Christian walk, and believed that if I did a good job for God, I would go to heaven when my time came. Let's call it earning my way to heaven. Now my wife knew that I was somewhat stubborn and that telling me different would only result in my not listening to her. So she decided to pray for me. She prayed every day for a whole year for me, and nothing changed in me. Two years, then three, and all the way to seven years. In the seventh year, I was walking down the street where there was a Bible bookstore, and without any thinking I walked in and asked if they had a Bible that didn't have all the *thee*s and *thou*s in it. The lady showed me a Living Bible, and it looked OK, and I bought it. I thought, what did I do that for? Then an idea came, and I gave it to my wife as a Christmas present. She opened it and looked at me and didn't say anything but "Thanks."

BORN AGAIN

One day, a few weeks after Christmas, I was unable to get to a church meeting because of a snowstorm. I was pacing about the house, and then I picked up this Living Bible and browsed through the Old Testament. I found several war stories that I enjoyed reading. I realized that I had an intense desire in me to read this Bible, so I decided to begin at Genesis and read the whole Bible—I did it in nine months. About seven months into reading it, I read Ephesians 2:8–9, which said, "For by grace are you saved through faith; and that not of yourselves: it is the gift of God. Not of works, lest any man should boast." This sure didn't line up with my thinking of earning my way to heaven. I figured this was a misprint. We had a few other versions of the Bible in the house, so I looked them up and found that the wording was different, but the meaning was the same. I then realized I was mistaken, and somehow I knew that I simply had to ask Jesus to come into my life and I would be born again—I did just that.

PURCHASING BOOKS ON THE HOLY SPIRIT

Within a few months of inviting Jesus into my heart, I accidently came across a program on television called '*the 700 Club*' and enjoyed listening to it. One night someone was being interviewed and shared about being baptised in the Holy Ghost and speaking in tongues. I was convinced that tongues had disappeared hundreds of years ago, so I decided that I would prove this fellow to be incorrect, and I wrote down all the scriptures that he gave. To my astonishment, everything he said was in my Bible, and I read the part before and after to make sure it was not taken out of context. One scripture stuck in my mind, and it was from Acts 1:8, "When the Holy Spirit comes upon you, you will receive power to be my witnesses in Jerusalem, in Judea and Samaria and to the ends of the earth." I wanted that power to witness. I prayed for myself, and nothing happened. So I went to that Bible bookstore where I had purchased the Living Bible from and asked if they had any books on the baptism of the Holy Spirit, and to my amazement they did; at that time, there was only about three dozen in the store. I couldn't make up my mind which one to buy, so I bought one of every book they had in the store. In the following few months, my wife and I read nearly all of them. We prayed for each other, and again nothing happened.

BAPTISED IN THE HOLY SPIRIT

About this time, we were invited to join two other couples and meet every Saturday night and have a Bible study. One night, a sister of one of the wives was there, and shared about the baptism of the Holy Spirit, and I was really interested. We found out that she and her husband and children were going to be at a place close to where we were going to vacation, and we arranged to get together on a certain date. We did that and spent the whole day helping them build a dock. At night-time, we sat around the fire, and we asked them to pray for us to receive the baptism of the Holy Spirit. They did, and let me share what happened! My wife, Bonnie, said she was experiencing an abundance of peace, and I was shaking all over, with the witness of the Holy Spirit going through me from my head to my toes, and it took about ten minutes. Bonnie had an out-of-body experience and was up high and looking down at us. Prior to this, she had an extremely sore back, and I had to help her get out of bed in the morning. When she came back into her body, she was completely healed. She experienced the speaking in tongues before I did, and prayed in the Spirit all night.

HEALED OF SUGAR DIABETES

I was a changed person and on fire for the Lord and would witness to many people. I realized that there must be many areas that I have misunderstood, and I asked the Lord to reveal them to me. This began to happen over the next few months. We joined a combined Catholic-Protestant prayer meeting, and we decided to take part in their class on the Holy Spirit. When the class was complete many weeks later, we were invited to come upstairs to the front of this Catholic church to be prayed for the baptism of the Holy Spirit. One of the leaders knew that we had been filled with the Holy Spirit, so when they stood in front of me and prayed, the Holy Spirit said to them to tell me I could have anything we wanted, and as I had sugar diabetes, I asked to be healed of it, and Bonnie didn't pray for herself but that I would be healed of sugar diabetes, and sure enough, I was healed, and it was confirmed by the doctor.

LOOKING AT FARMS

Sometime after this, we were encouraged to form our own prayer meeting, and we saw many healings and miracles take place and lives changed. The core group was made up of two couples and the two of us. It was at this time that the Holy Spirit was dealing with us to believe for a farm, not near where we lived in Windsor, but in the area of Owen Sound, Ontario, which is about two and a half hours north-west of Toronto. I arranged to meet a real estate broker, and this person spent two days with me looking at hobby farms. At the end of the first day of looking at farms, she gave me the information on seven more farms we would see the next day. I spent the first night in our trailer in a trailer park near Owen Sound, and I made up a sheet of paper with all the farms on it and columns to itemize what each farm contained. One farm had a fieldstone house, and I remember thinking that they should take a bulldozer and tear it down. Something unusual happened that night—about every hour on the hour, I awoke and saw a vision of that fieldstone house with about fifty acres with it. My attitude towards antique things, including older houses, changed that night, and I could hardly wait to see it.

I asked the real estate person if we could see that farm right away. She explained that she had set up appointments at different times during the day and that one was the last. During the latter part of the day, we could not find it, and the real estate lady suggested we skip it. I said, "No, let's go over the instructions and find it." And we did. It had a lot of potential, and I could see that we could have a pond and a garden area and many other things. I prayed about the price and got $62,000 from the Holy Spirit. The asking price was $79,000. I brought my wife and our two daughters to see it. We all liked it, and I asked the real estate lady to make an offer on our behalf of $62,000. She felt the price was way too low and did not want to make the offer. However, she eventually did, and the owners were quite upset with her.

BUYING THE FARM

From time to time we would drive past it and think that someday we would own it. By the fall of that year, the owners dropped the price to $70,000, and I said to the Holy Spirit, "Thanks, I can now negotiate it. We are at $62,000, and they are at $70,000." The Holy Spirit said to me, "You have a decision to make—you either go My way or yours." I said, "What is Your way?" And I received the answer, "$62,000." So I didn't do anything. In the spring it went back on the market at $70,000, and someone made an offer to buy it at $70,000, and it got sold. My wife and I had prayed every day for us to get it, and here we were a year later and had lost it. The Holy Spirit asked me what we were praying, and I said, "For the farm that God has for us near Owen Sound." And the Holy Spirit said, "Keep praying that." We did, and the real estate lady had us come and look at some farms, but they were not what we wanted.

Finally before the Civic Holiday in August, we got a call about another farm and saw it right after the holiday weekend. It was eighty-six acres, had three ponds, had a large woods, and had six bedrooms upstairs and one downstairs. I had noticed a women's *Aglow* pamphlet in one of the bedrooms and wondered if they were Christians or not. I asked if I could come back the next day and have the owner take me through the woods. We did this, and it turned out that they were Christians. I explained that we wanted to turn it into a retreat centre and grow things on the farm organically. That got their interest. They were asking $89,000 for the farm, and we said that the farm was probably worth it, but we couldn't go past $70,000 and that we would need to get a mortgage on it of $25,000—the problem was that interest rates were at 20% then. It was out of the question. A few days later we heard from the real estate lady, and she said that they could get us a loan of $25,000 at 12% and would we go at $79,000. I prayed about it, and the Holy Spirit told me to ask them how much they would have to pay up front to get the $25,000 at 12% and then deduct it from the $79,000 and go at that price. We found out that they would have to pay $7,000 up front to get it, and we said, "We know you wanted to help us, but would you consider taking the $7,000 off the $79,000 and accept $72,000 for the farm?" They agreed, and we purchased the farm and got our own loan for the $25,000.

It's interesting how the Holy Spirit worked on our behalf for us to get the farm. I asked the Holy Spirit why we were not to go over $62,000 for the other farm and were told that we had prayed for this farm and that it would go on the market in the fall. We rented out the barn to a neighbour and the house to another neighbour, and the income from that was equal to our payments at the bank. Then within four months I lost my job, but the income paid for the loan, and we did not lose the farm. God took care of that. Where would we have been if it had not been for the Holy Spirit?

BLADDER INFECTION

The other day, I was thinking about the time Bonnie and I were in Maui and she came down with a bladder infection. She had a chronic bladder infection problem and would get a bladder infection nearly every month. The doctor said, "Take the big red pills for a week, and it will clear up." In Maui, she took the bladder pills for one week, and then a couple of days later, she had another bladder infection. We had no more red pills, and as you know, it is hard to get prescribed medication in another country. When I had wakened up that particular morning and realized that Bonnie was in the bathroom with another bladder infection, I prayed and asked God what to do under the circumstances. This was about the time we were just beginning to hear the voice of the Lord, and I sensed that I should get her back into bed and pray for her. She said, "Make it a quick prayer," and I did, something like "I ask you, Lord, to heal this bladder infection and in the name of Jesus." That was it. She seemed to have quickly fallen asleep or, as we call it, slain in the Spirit. She slept for an hour, and upon waking, all the symptoms were gone, and I believe it was twenty years before she had another bladder infection. Praise be to the Lord, and thank you for the Holy Spirit.

YOUTH GROUP IN OUR CHURCH

In the early seventies, we got involved in leading the youth in our church. We used to go to the beach or go horseback riding or some other event every couple of weeks and then have a Bible study. Eventually, all the kids became born again, and we emphasised prayer and honesty and righteous living. We were approached by some of the kids and were asked if we knew anything about the baptism in the Holy Spirit and speaking in tongues. We said yes and began to teach them about this. Then we arranged a retreat up in Michigan with a Spirit-filled doctor and some of the boys that he worked with. Saturday night, everyone got filled with the Holy Spirit and began speaking in tongues. What a time we had. We found out later that a couple of the boys had brought a 40-ounce bottle of whiskey and were going to drink it. The power and conviction of the Holy Spirit was so strong that they dumped the whole bottle down the drain. One fellow in the group was excellent at stealing things in stores and never had gotten caught; he was delivered that night by the Holy Spirit and stopped the bad habit.

Anyways, when we got home and the kids started telling their parents how they could speak in tongues, we began to have telephone calls, and we explained to the parents what the Bible said about this. Then the parents began telephoning the pastor and not getting anywhere, then started telephoning the bishop over the whole district. Most of this we knew nothing about. It was like the Holy Spirit protected us, and the kids really grew in the Holy Spirit and began using the gifts of the Spirit. We had another retreat the next year in June at a trailer camp and with the use of a barn (the upper floor with a little hay on it) for our meeting room. I remember at the end of the Saturday night one of the speakers said to me, "Norm, take this fellow over there and pray for him to receive the baptism in the Holy Spirit." When I went to pray for him, I could not speak in English, but only in tongues, so I put my hand on his head and spoke in tongues very loudly for about ten minutes. He got baptised in the Holy Spirit and spoke in tongues.

I found out later that he got delivered of drinking alcoholic beverages, delivered of drugs, and had made the decision to go to a Spirit-filled seminar and become a pastor. He did this, and years later, he shared with us how the Holy Spirit led him to go to Indonesia and start over forty churches there. He started a church in Seattle and even went to start churches in Japan. How did all this happen? It was the Holy Spirit working.

CHAPTER 2

What's Next?

I would like to share with you a few testimonies of God's blessings.

GOD'S DESIRE—A BUICK RIVIERA

In 1974 we were driving an old Buick. We were working with the youth in our church, and it was suggested that we consider using a trailer camp and a barn for our next retreat in June. We checked it out and made arrangements to have the retreat there. It was a great retreat with many signs and wonders happening. Prior to the retreat, we pulled our seventeen-foot house trailer up to the trailer camp. On our way home from the trailer camp, our old Buick died in the middle of a town called Arthur. We sold it for $200 and rented a car to get home. Amazingly, on the Friday, before the retreat, my boss enquired whether I would be interested in getting a company car. Well, when I returned to work on Monday, I told my boss that we were definitely interested in a company car. My boss suggested that I get a rental car for a few months and then enter into a leasing agreement in the fall for three years. We liked a certain make of car and arranged to rent it until the fall. For some unknown reason, we had many repairs to make on this temporary rental car and did not want one of those for three years. Bonnie and I decided to pray about what car we should ask for. At the time, I received nothing, but Bonnie said, "I don't understand what a vacation spot would have to do with your car." I said, "What do you mean?" And she said, "I keep getting the word Riviera." I was all excited because that was my favourite car and I had not spoken it to Bonnie. We then began to believe for it. Basically, it was a more expensive car and not just a company car. When the time came to order a car in the fall, my boss asked me if I wanted to get the same car as I had temporarily rented, and I said no and said my desire would be a Buick Riviera, and he didn't know what that was, and when I explained that the president of a company we dealt with had one, he said, "Oh. Leave it with me." And next day he said, "I talked with my wife about it, and she said, 'Get Norm the car.'" We leased that Buick for four years.

HOW GOD BROUGHT A LINCOLN CONTINENTIAL MARK V FOR US

Now, eighteen months before that lease was up, the Buick was going through the car wash, and something happened. It was the kind of car wash where you exit the car and they attach a hook to the car and it is pulled down the line. I walked down the hall and stood at the far end to watch the car come down the line as I normally do. All of a sudden the car became a Lincoln Continental, and I was totally surprised. I looked away and then back, and still the same. It went through the soaping cycle, then the rinse cycle, and then the air-blowing cycle to dry it, and it came to where I was standing, and then only after the employee took the hook off the car did it turn back into the Buick. I asked the Lord what that was all about. The Holy Spirit told me if I would believe for a Lincoln Continental, He would cause it to happen. I struggled with that, as I was the comptroller and not the owner of the company. But as I continued to call it in and believe for God to do it, I could picture it in my mind and spirit. I eventually came to the point in my spirit that I knew it was going to come in one day.

Then the time came, and the lease on the Buick was shortly running out. My boss said to me, "Do you want to get another Buick?"

And I said, "There is a car that I would love to get and drive." He asked me what it was, and I said a Lincoln Continental, and he was, I think, very surprised. He got back to me the next day and said, "Go order it." Now the company was in the process of negotiating the sale of the company to a firm in Guelph. I reasoned with myself that it would not be good to have them buy the company and then find out that the comptroller had just leased a Lincoln Continental. So I said to God, "I ask you to go before me, and I will ask their permission to lease it, and I will tell them that even if they don't approve it, I will work for them and do a good job."

A week or so later, they asked me to come to Guelph, and I flew from Windsor to Toronto. One of the owners picked me up at the Toronto airport, and I explained to him that the present owner had approved the leasing of the car, but I would not do it unless they approved it. He said, "Leave it with me." We were in meetings for most of the day, and at the end of the day, he explained he could not drive me to the airport and someone else would do it. Then he said, "By the way, go ahead and order that Lincoln Continental." On the inside of me, I said, "Thank you, God. You are wonderful!"

Many times as I tell these stories, I say I am sharing this story not to brag on me but to brag on my God. He wants to richly bless His children, and I find that many Christians won't let him and will not believe what they hear—either from lack of knowledge of the Word of God or total unbelief that God would do that for them. I realize, of course, that many Christians have not learned how to hear the voice of the Lord. There are many books out today on how to learn how to hear God's voice. We so enjoyed driving that car and sharing how God brought it about.

LENDING THE LINCOLN CONTINENTAL TO A FACTORY WORKER

We had a friend who worked in a factory in Kitchener, Ontario, and he drove us to the airport, and we said to him, "You keep the car while we are away, and you must drive it to work every day." Well, his fellow employees were quite surprised that someone who drove a Lincoln Continental would lend it to a factory worker. It was a great witness for the Lord, because he told them we were Christians. There was another situation that was interesting. One day my wife was driving it, and just in front of the local hospital was a lady (a nurse) standing in the rain waiting for a bus. It was cold and damp, so Bonnie stopped and said, "Can I give you a lift somewhere?" And she said, "OK." When she was let out of the car, she said, "I thought people who drove these kind of cars were stuck up and would never pick up someone like me." Of course Bonnie had shared with her that we were Christians.

FORD MUSTANG

Now, let me backtrack a couple of years. It was Wednesday, July 1, and I was walking across a field at our farm. The Holy Spirit came all over me, and I sensed Him saying, "I have a surprise for you." I immediately asked, "What is the surprise?" Then I saw a picture of our children shaking Christmas presents and asking what they were. Obviously, we would not tell them and spoil the surprise, so the Holy Spirit was saying to me, "Don't ask me as it will spoil the surprise." I began to thank God for the surprise, even though I didn't know what it was. On Saturday morning, July 4, one of our daughters was home and received a call from the head office of Pepsi Cola asking for Mr. Weber. She said, "He is away up north at our farm." And they said, "Tell him he just won a brand-new Ford Mustang and call our number so that arrangements could be made for him to come to our head office and be presented with the keys to the new Ford Mustang." Arrangements were made, and we got a brand-new spanking Ford Mustang. Just think about this, God told me on the Wednesday about the surprise, and it happened on the following Saturday. I understand there were several thousand tickets and only ours was picked out. Does that make me lucky? No! That's my God in action, and it can be yours too, if you believe.

SALE OF SHARES

Some years prior to our buying the farm, the Holy Spirit spoke to my wife and said that if we believe, God would bring a very large amount of money into our hands. As you can guess, my wife and I were very excited. But as the weeks went by, I was trying to figure out how all this would happen, and I could not figure it out. This may sound foolish, but I stopped praying for it. The following Saturday, both my wife and I were in the kitchen, and I looked at her, and the tears were flowing down her face, and I said, "What is wrong?" She said the Holy Spirit had just spoken to her and that the Holy Spirit said, "If you and Norm do not agree and call in this large sum of money, you will never see it." Well, I guess I was like David in the Bible. I was quick to repent and began to thank and call in the large amount of money.

Months went by, and a year and a half later, my boss said to me that as he was approaching the age of 63; he was looking for a buyer for the company. For information purposes, he allowed me to purchase shares in the company, and when I would get my yearly bonus, we would spend half of it on a vacation and put the other half into shares in the company. My brother, also a CA, cautioned me about buying shares in a private company as you cannot just go and sell them in the marketplace, but I somehow knew that this was what I should do. So my boss said to me, "I want you to keep this matter of selling the company confidential and to expect that different companies would come in and look at it." And I was to explain the financials, our budgets, and our marketing plan.

So over the months, different companies came in, and I did my part. About fifteen months into this, a company from Guelph told me that next week, they were going to present a letter of intent to purchase the company. They did, and thus began weeks of negotiations and questions by lawyers, etc. The purchase price was rather complicated and began with the yearend book value (still six months away), adjusted for one-half of the difference between the appraised value of the land, buildings, and equipment to the fixed asset value on the books, plus many other calculations.

Eight months later, we were in the lawyer's office and all sitting around a big table. Each of the items in the calculation of the purchase price were presented and tabulated, and after several hours, we then had the selling price of the shares of the company. I took my calculator and divided the selling price by the number of shares and got a selling price per share and multiplied by the number of shares I held, and it came out to exactly what the Lord had told my wife two years earlier. Wow, what a God we serve. I could hardly wait to get home and share all this with my wife. We rejoiced together and thanked our God. We tithed off this amount, went on a mission's trip to the Philippines, and purchased an eighty-six-acre farm. Can you imagine God knowing ahead of time what the selling price of my shares would be two years down the road? But that's God. As you guessed, I like bragging on Him.

THE VACATION THAT GOD PICKED OUT

Vacations—let me tell you some stories about vacations. When the children were small, we pulled a seventeen-foot house trailer to Florida. Actually, we went all the way down to the Keys and stayed at different camps. While we were there, our youngest daughter became quite sick, and we had to take her to the hospital. Our other daughter also got sick, and then I got sick on the trip home. We drove over a thousand miles in snowy conditions and on icy roads pulling a house trailer. When we got home, we were all exhausted. Now before we left for this vacation, my wife said to me, "Do you think this is God's plan for our vacation?" And I said, "I don't know, and I don't think it matters." It did matter. We decided that we would never again go on vacation without praying about it. We followed the habit of taking our children one year on vacation and leaving them home with someone the next year.

We prayed about where to go on vacation and saw a huge letter *M* made out of wood, and this was the first letter of the place where we were to go. So I went to the travel agent and picked up brochures on different vacation places, and then we began to search through it.

We eventually came to the brochure with the name of an island called Maui. I had thought that all these islands were just part of Hawaii. To my surprise, I found out they all had different names.

We contacted the travel agent and said we wanted to go to Maui for two weeks for the two of us. The travel agent tried to talk us into going to the main island for a time and then to several of the other islands. We said no, we only want to go to Maui. Maui has one of the best beaches in the world, and we enjoyed it. It was during this trip that Bonnie had the two bladder infections as commented on in Chapter 1.

UNDERSTANDING THE STILL SMALL VOICE OF THE HOLY SPIRIT

This was the time that gas rationing was in effect, and I had to go early to the gas station and get gas. Then the Holy Spirit directed me to drive up a mountain (actually a large hill). These were sandy roads and went through the sugar cane plantations and climbed until you reached the top of the hill. The Holy Spirit directed me to walk into a field at the top where there were shrubs growing. He began to enlighten me on the desire he put in me to grow tea roses and how I hoed them, pruned them, fertilized them, and even picked them for my wife. But He said to me, "There is one thing you have never done, and that is to bend over and smell the rosebud." God was right—I had never done that. He spoke to me in a different way than before, what we call the still, small voice. Then he said to me, "I want you to start getting up an hour earlier and spend time in my Word." And I made that decision then. God was about to test me on this new method of hearing his voice.

The sandy road I had come up was very bumpy, and I decided to use another road to get down the large hill. One looked good, and I took it. But before long, I slammed on the brakes because the ditch on my right crisscrossed the road and blocked my way. Trying to back up on a sloping road didn't work, and I was at least ten miles from the main road. What do I do? I decided to pray this new way and listen to the Holy Spirit. He said, "Drive the car into the ditch [which was about three feet deep], and I will bring you out on the other side." I drove it into the ditch, and it bounced out on the other side. The sand was red, and I had on white shorts, white top, and white socks; I now had red shorts, red top, and red socks. As I drove down the sandy road, I again had to slam on the brakes as the ditch now crossed the road going the other way. I prayed about it, and the Holy Spirit said, "Do the same." The ditch was now about four feet deep. I drove into the ditch and bounced out on the other side. Rejoicing, I drove back to the motel.

LEARNING TO HEAR THE VOICE OF THE LORD

My wife and I were baptised in the Holy Spirit in 1973. We had heard about people being led of the Holy Spirit, or as some say, hearing the voice of God. At times we felt that maybe God was speaking to us about something and leading us to do something, but we weren't sure. Every year, we would go to Troy, Michigan, which is just north of Detroit, for the annual Full Gospel Business Men's Regional Convention. It was held in a parking lot of a very large hotel. The tent held 5,000 people and from time to time, the sides of the tent were opened and chairs put outside the tent so that an additional 1,000 people could sit there. It ran from Thursday to Saturday. That particular year, we had enjoyed Thursday, Friday, and Saturday morning meetings. It was now Saturday afternoon, and Kenneth Hagin Sr. was the speaker. He started off by saying that he wasn't too sure what he was to speak on and shared a few thoughts. Then he announced that the Spirit of the Lord had just spoken to him and he would teach on how to hear the voice of the Lord. Well, you can imagine our excitement!

MORE ON HEARING THE VOICE OF THE LORD—THE WITNESS OF THE HOLY SPIRIT

He shared how the Holy Spirit had shown him that there were three primary ways that God, by His Holy Spirit, speaks to us. First, there is the inward witness or witness of the Spirit, which is explained in Romans 8:16, "The spirit itself bears witness with our spirit, that we are the children of God," and in Hebrews 10:15, "Whereof the Holy Ghost also is a witness to us." He explained that we now have biblical base for the witness of the Holy Spirit. He further commented on Proverbs 20:27, "The spirit of man is the candle of the Lord, searching all the inward parts of the belly." He explained that this last scripture means God will enlighten us; He will guide us through our spirits. The witness of the Holy Spirit is like the anointing of God, somewhat like pins and needles. The Bible does not say that the body of man is the candle of the Lord, nor that the mind of man is the candle of the Lord. It says that the spirit of man is the candle of the Lord.

THE DEVELOPMENT OF FOLLOWING THE HOLY SPIRIT

Kenneth Hagin Sr. further explained that the Holy Spirit encourages us, tells us thing to come, nudges us, and prods us. When the witness of the Spirit comes, pray in the Spirit, focus on the Lord, be quiet before Him, say out loud or under your breath what you are receiving—if it is correct, the witness of the Spirit continues; if wrong, it diminishes and stops. Once this is developed, it will become a reliable means of divine direction. But in the beginning, you must be careful and check out important direction with other Spirit-led believers or your pastor, if he moves in the Holy Spirit, until you have fully developed this gift of God. It can take some time. All leading must line up with the Word of God. God will not lead you to do something that is contrary to His Word.

WHAT IT'S LIKE TO WALK WITH THE HOLY SPIRIT

THE STILL, SMALL VOICE, OR INWARD VOICE

The second method is called the still, small voice, or inward voice. It is a little harder to discern, but it is a method that many Christians use. The inward man is a spirit man and has a voice, just as the actual man has a voice. You will be surprised at what the Bible calls it. Romans 9:1 says, "I say the truth in Christ, I lie not, my conscience also bearing me witness in the Holy Ghost." We hear in the World, "Let your conscience be your guide." Is your conscience a safe guide? Yes and no! Let's look at 2 Corinthians 5:17, "Therefore if any man be in Christ, he is a new creature [a brand-new man in Christ]: old things are passed away [the nature of the devil in one's spirit is gone]; all things have become new [in his spirit he has the nature of God]."

There is a need to walk in holiness. The still, small voice, or inward voice, comes as an inward impression or a hunch. It is best to be apart from the world and be in a time of prayer. We have to be careful and not accept every impression as from God, but discern it. Some people call this developing the human spirit.

A PITCHER OF ORANGE JUICE

The third method is called the audible voice of God. The scriptural base comes from 1 Samuel 3:4–10, wherein God spoke out loud to Samuel and he thought it was Eli talking to him, and Eli said it was not him. Again it happened, and Eli said it was not him. The third time, Eli told Samuel to say, "Speak, Lord; for thy servant heareth."

There are a lot of stories relating to the farm. We had purchased it in the fall of 1982, and the following summer we spent a week's vacation there. I woke up early on the Sunday morning. As I was having trouble going back to sleep, I prayed in the Spirit, and I received a direction from the Holy Spirit to take a large jug of orange juice and go into the twenty-five-acre woods via the pathway at the corner of the two roads. This seemed strange to me, and I asked the question why. The Holy Spirit said, "There is a motorcycle gang sleeping on the pathway in the woods, and as they have nothing to drink, I want you to take them the jug of orange juice and tell them that I instructed you to do this, and then leave."

I thought maybe I was imagining this and then thought even if I had it wrong, it would be a nice walk on an early Sunday morning. So I mixed up the orange juice and walked down the road to the corner with the other road and walked into the woods on the pathway. After about five minutes, I turned a corner, and to my astonishment, there were several motorcycles and then several sleeping bags with men sleeping in them. The hair on the back of my neck rose straight up, and my breath came fast. I just stood there. I remember someone telling me years ago that if I did whatever the Lord instructed me, He would take care of me. So I said out very loud, "Good morning, fellows. God spoke to me before I got out of bed this morning and told me to bring you this jug of orange juice as you didn't have anything to drink. Enjoy it and goodbye." I turned around and walked away down the pathway, shaking all over. There have been a few times in my life when I have missed what the Holy Spirit has said, but it is really exciting when you obey and follow through.

GOD PLANNED FOR US TO HAVE A ROOT CELLAR

A few years after this orange juice experience, I went to a Full Gospel Business Men's Fellowship Advance in Peterborough at Trent University in early June. I meet a fellow that lived close to where I lived, and made friends with him. Later on in the year, we made plans to be at the farmhouse for the Christmas season, and I invited this fellow and his mother to join us for dinner. In the evening he and I were sitting in the living room, talking. He had a portable sawmill that he could make logs from the woods and cut up into lumber. He wanted to build a small building where he could heat and store lumber in so that it wouldn't warp. So I said, "Why don't we ask the Holy Spirit how to do it." We prayed, and I got dimensions on a building and information about this building. The dimensions were six feet wide and twenty feet long and consisting of two rooms. I saw four-inch plastic pipes coming into each room; on one end of the room, the pipe came near the floor, and at the other end of the room, the pipe started at the ceiling. This fellow began to laugh and laugh as he realized I didn't know that it was something else. He said, "Ask the Holy Spirit what this building is for." It seemed like a redundant question, but I did anyways and got the answer, "A winter storage cellar."

With this, the fellow fell on the floor and laughed and laughed as he knew I didn't have a clue what this was all about. He said, "Norm, you have the dimensions of a root cellar." And I said with a question mark on my face, "Am I going to grow roots in this building?" It took this fellow ten minutes before he could stop laughing and talk to me. He explained that a root cellar is built in the ground and a couple of feet of earth over the top and with vents to allow air to come in and go out. And if it is built correctly, it does not freeze inside and stays at a few degrees above freezing, and all without electricity. Knowing that the Lord wanted me to build one, I purchased a book on root cellars and had one built to the exact specifications I had gotten from the Holy Spirit. From reading the book I found out that apples and potatoes cannot be stored in the same room as the apples give off a gas that causes the potatoes to prematurely bud. So the following year when we stored potatoes in the separate room, they would not bud until the following June and still be firm and in good condition. The apples were stored in the other room and lasted a long time.

HEALING OF CANCER IN THE NECK'S LYMPH NODES

I was just thinking the other day about a time when we were teaching from our manual on how to heal the sick, and a lady called the pastor and asked if someone could come out to their home and pray for her mother, who had cancer in the neck's lymph nodes. The call was directed to us, and we contacted the lady. We decided that in light of the fact that the lady's husband did not believe in healing, we should pray for the person in our home. So the lady at church and her mother came to our home for the evening.

We like to share stories of how other people were healed and build up their faith for healing. We also shared scriptures on healing and explained it to them. We shared with them the scripture from Mark 11:23, which says, "For verily I SAY unto you, that whosoever shall SAY unto this mountain. Be thou removed, and be thou cast into the sea; and shall not doubt in his heart, but shall believe that those things which he SAITH shall come to pass: he shall have whatsoever he SAITH." We explained that this was not praying to God, but rather speaking to the problem, whatever that would be, and believing what you said. We mixed this with the laying on of hands as stated Mark 16:18, which says, "They shall lay hands on the sick, and they shall recover." So we laid hands on her neck, where the cancer was, and then spoke to the cancer and commanded it to die and come out of her body. Her neck was quite swollen where the cancer was. We explained to her that she needed to speak to the cancer every day until the swelling went down.

The lady came with her daughter two weeks later to our church, and we noticed a glow on her face. She told us that she was commanding the cancer to leave every day, and she stated, "I just know that it is going to leave and be gone." We saw her again in church in another two weeks, and the swelling had gone down a little bit. Weeks and weeks went by, and we never saw her again. On New Year's Day, we received a call from the daughter to say hello and thanks. We asked, "What happened to your mother?" She said, "Didn't she call you? A few weeks after you saw her in church, all the swelling had gone down, and she went to her doctor, who could find no cancer." So she came home, and she and her husband went to Florida for the winter. Exciting, eh?

EXTENDED LAYING ON OF HANDS AND PRAYING IN THE HOLY SPIRIT

We taught in a Christian camp up near Parry Sound for a week, and there was a woman from Sri Lanka who was there and was suffering from knee problems. She could barely bend her legs and was scheduled for surgery on both knees. Her relatives who accompanied her did not believe in God's healing power. We prayed for her with the laying on of hands, and in this situation we were led by the Holy Spirit to keep our hands on her knees for some time. She felt a heat in her knees. She described it as a deep heat like rubbing ointment. The warmth stayed until the middle of the night. By next morning she was running up and down the stairs, testifying of God's faithfulness to heal! Her relatives who came with her were simply amazed to see her walking and running normally. We have seen many situations as these where God demonstrated His healing power.

Chapter 3

Carrying On

GOD'S WISH FOR OUR DAUGHTER, CHERYL, TO GO TO ORAL ROBERTS UNIVERSITY

One of our daughters, Cheryl, works for a Christian ministry 100 Huntley Street in Burlington, Ontario. She is a TV producer and from time to time travels the world and reports. During her grade 12 high school class, I was reading a Christian magazine published in the United States. I came across an article on Oral Roberts University. It invited potential students to come, free of charge, to Oral Roberts University for the Easter weekend in March. I felt the Holy Spirit leading me to fill it out and put Cheryl's name in it. I did not tell her what I had done. Weeks later, she received an invitation personally made out to her to come, at no charge, for the Easter weekend and explore their programs. She read it all and said to my wife, Bonnie, and I, "I would like to go to Tulsa, Oklahoma, and explore the programs of Oral Roberts University." Arrangements were made, and my wife and I and our other daughter went with her. She thoroughly enjoyed the weekend, and upon returning home, she decided to attend for four years studying media. She has been in Christian ministry since she graduated years ago.

I often thought what would have become of her if I had not filled out that invitation for her to go to Oral Roberts University. Or I have thought what would have happened if I had not learned how to follow the leading of the Holy Spirit.

APPLE CIDER PRESS

Now, another story about the farm. We were taking apples to a farm that pressed them into apple cider, but we really needed a press situated in our barn. I heard of a company in Buffalo, New York, that made them, so I called them and said, "Do you take trade-ins, and do you have any?" I explained that I lived in Ontario, Canada. They told me that for sales in Canada, they do not take trade-ins but would subsequently contact me if someone was upgrading their apple press and had an existing one for sale. Sure enough, a couple of months later, they called me and gave me an address of a farm east of Oshawa, which is some four to five hours away. I had received the information in the middle of the winter, and I did not want to drive all that distance. I talked to the farmer, and he explained what he had and said it was in good shape. I prayed about it and asked the Holy Spirit what to do. I received a word from the Lord through the Holy Spirit that it was in good shape and the farmer was a Christian and could be trusted. So I went to my bank with my cheque and got it certified and sent it to the farmer and said, "I talked with someone who knows you, and they told me I could trust you. Will you hold the press until the spring, and I will have someone contact you and pick it up." He said yes, and in the spring a friend of mine picked it up and brought it to the our farm, and it turned out to be in good shape, and we used it every year since then to make many gallons of apple cider and froze it.

CUTTING GRASS IN ORCHARDS

On our farm, we have two apple orchards, one we call the old orchard, about two acres, and the new orchard, about seven acres. We grow the apples organically. We mow the grass in the rows with our tractor and bush hog, but we have nothing to cut the grass between the trees. This last year, a dear friend of mine who lives two hours away rounded up several guys, and they came with riding mowers and weed eaters and cut all the grass between the trees. It was such a blessing and made the orchards look like parks.

INSTALLING OUTSIDE LIGHTS

The outside lights on our home had gotten damaged and needed replacement. Bonnie felt led by the Holy Spirit to go and buy three outside lights to replace the ones we had. Within hours of buying these outside lights, a friend of ours who lived five hours away called and said he and his wife wanted to come and visit us. This fellow was an electrician and installed the lights and set up the motion adjustments so if one came on, the other two did also. Thank you, Lord.

TRIP ON FLIGHT 666

Many of us have read about the fact that we might someday be required to have the number 666 put on us to buy or sell in the end days. Well, we went on a trip to Mexico, and the flight number was 666. Let me tell you the story. The flight was out of Windsor, Ontario, and direct to Mexico. We had someone drop us off at the airport with our luggage in the late afternoon. Our plane came in from Jamaica, but they would not let us board. The RCMP boarded the plane with their sniffer dogs and found drugs. We were supposed to have dinner on the plane, but as we were delayed for hours, they told us we could eat in the airport restaurant, and one hundred and fifty people went for supper. They ran out of food, and then they told us to come back in the morning at seven thirty and they would have a plane for us. We came back to the airport at seven thirty but no plane. They selected another plane in Toronto, and as it was being fuelled, it was damaged by the fuel truck and could not fly. So they arranged to get another plane out of Montreal, but with ice, etc., the plane was delayed several hours.

Finally, we got on the plane, and it landed safely in Mexico, but the power was out, so they could not bring the luggage to the terminal. They directed us to a bus parked some distance away, and as we went to the bus and stood in line to get on, it rained heavily, and most of us got drenched. The bus that we boarded had its air conditioning on, and they couldn't turn it off, and we froze. Finally, we got to the hotel in Cancun, and after waiting some time, they gave us the key to our room. When we got to our room, there was one huge bed, and with our two children, that was not satisfactory, and we had to go back and demand another room. We then went to this room, and when we opened the door, the room was flooded with water. Apparently, when the power went off, someone was taking a shower and simply left the towel in the shower so that when the power came on and the shower came on, the towel blocked the water from going into the drain, and it flooded the room.

So downstairs we went again and had an employee come with us. She opened the sliding doors and with a large mop pushed the water out through the sliding doors down the front of the hotel. When the lady finally finished, we all laid on the beds and laughed and laughed. This was flight 666.

GOD DECIDED WE NEEDED A WATER RAM

Have you heard of a water ram? I hadn't. In one of my quiet times with the Lord, He said to me to have a water ram installed on the farm. So I said, "Lord, bring someone who can tell me what it is." A couple of weeks later, an elderly couple pulled up in the driveway and said that many years ago they owned the farm and began telling us about the farm then. They said they had a water ram down in the valley, and we said, "Tell us what it is." So they said, "If you have water running downhill and can direct it into a water ram, the pressure of the water going downhill will build up pressure in the attached water pressure tank, and this pressure can be used to move the water hundreds of feet even uphill." So I then said, "Lord, now tell me where I can get it." A couple of weeks later, we met a fellow who lived nearby and told us that his brother lived north of Guelph and that across the road there were Mennonite people who had a water ram. So we arranged to visit this brother the next time we were in the area. The brother took us across the road and introduced us to the Mennonite farmer. He took us across the field to where there was a stream, and from the stream ran a pipe downhill to a small block building about six feet by six feet. Inside the building was the ram, and it was operating, and every few seconds it spewed out water inside the building, and at the same time, pressure was building up in the pressure tank. I took pictures and asked all kinds of questions. Then I asked them where they got it, and they told me the directions to a fellow Mennonite farmer who built it. We then drove to this fellow's farm, and there was horse and buggies and also a block building with a hydro line coming into it—this was a machine shop. The fellow was home and took us to the block building and showed us a brochure where we could buy the water ram in the United States.

BUILDING THE WATER RAM

He told me the price would be about $3,000. I couldn't understand why he was not offering to build one for me, so I asked the Lord what to do, and He said to me, "Share you testimony of how you got saved." And within minutes there was an opportunity to do such. He said, "Oh, you are a brother in the Lord. I will build you what you want." I asked the price, and he said, "500 Canadian dollars, and I only build them in the winter." As it was now September, I gave him $100 and said I would come in the spring and pick it up and pay him the balance. In the spring, I came with my trailer and picked it up and paid him. We purchased seventy feet of four-inch aluminium pipe and had someone build us a tank five feet wide and two feet high with a connection at the bottom to attach the four-inch pipe. We built the block building six feet by six feet and put the roof on it. Inside the building, we installed a drain pipe (eight inches in diameter) and made the cement floor drain into the drain pipe. From the pressure tank, we hooked up a ¾-inch ABS pipe and ran it a few hundred feet outside. Now we had to direct the water running out of our big pond into the five-foot-wide tank, and when the water and air ran downhill into the water ram, it began to work, and within ten minutes, we had water running out the ¾-inch ABS pipe. Now the Holy Spirit directed me to go and buy three coils of ¾ inch ABS pipe to give me 750 feet of hose and pipe and run it uphill to the silo and then up 25 feet on the silo and attach the hose. When I went back and got the water ram working, we had water coming out the hose at the top of the silo. Basically, the hose was 750 feet long and going uphill. I would estimate there is about a rise of about 70 feet from the valley to the top of the silo. We subsequently put a 50-gallon tank on top of the silo (incidentally, we don't use the silo).

DRIP SYSTEM

Now the Holy Spirit instructed that we were to install a drip system in the garden area and we would need a pressure of 15 psi at the bottom of the silo. I had attached the 2-inch hose coming out of the tank on top of the silo to a 1 ½-inch valve and then to a 1 inch and then to a ¾ valve and hose. But I only had 10 psi at the ground level. So I prayed about how to fix it, and the Holy Spirit instructed me to have the 2-inch hose come down to within a couple of feet from the ground and then go to 1 ½ inches, then to 1 inch, and then to ¾ inch, and then we had 15 psi at the ground.

ACQUIRING THE MATERIAL FOR THE DRIP SYSTEM

The next job was to purchase 3/8-thick hose with the drip built into it every thirteen inches. So I went to Leamington to the wholesale store that sold that kind of hose. I had a drawing made of what I needed, and the price on it was $1,000. That's a lot of money! So I again prayed about it, and the Holy Spirit said to come back here next Saturday at exactly 9:00 a.m. So next Saturday at 9:00 a.m., I was there, and they gave me a price again of about $1,000. I asked if they knew of where I could get used hose to do the job, and the salesman said, "Talk to the fellow behind you." This fellow said, "Follow me home, I have lots of it." He had lots of coils of it and all the connections also. It was exactly what I needed. I asked him for a price, and he said $75—I bought all of it. So when everything was hooked up, I had a drip system for the whole garden with water supplied by the water ram. Would you say, we serve a mighty God! When I reread some of these true stories, I am amazed even now on what God can do if we follow Him and do as He directs us.

INVITATION TO CHARLES AND FRANCIS HUNTER

Years ago, when the charismatic movement was in full swing in 1974 to 1978, all the prayer meetings were tied together, and I was involved in arranging for speakers to come and speak to the whole group. We felt in the Spirit that we were to invite Charles and Francis Hunter to come to Windsor. I wrote them a letter of invitation, and no response. I then said to the Lord, whatever it takes, I need to invite them to come to Windsor for a citywide meeting. After that, Bonnie and I felt that God wanted us to go to Montego Bay in Jamaica. We made arrangements and went with our two daughters.

MEETING REPRESENTATIVES OF MINISTRY OF CHARLES AND FRANCIS HUNTER

It was warm, and we enjoyed the beach and the pool. Near the end of our vacation, we heard there was to be a Christian meeting and speaker down the mountain at the sea level on Saturday. So we went to it. It was Spirit-filled, and we enjoyed it. There was one couple we enjoyed who came also from Canada, from the city of Calgary. After talking to them for some time, I asked them what they did in Calgary, and they said, "We are the Canadian representatives of Charles and Francis Hunter." Wow, were we excited, and when we explained about wanting them to come to Windsor, Ontario, they said, "We will have Francis call you this coming week." And guess what? Francis did call us. We talked about renting the city's Cleary

Auditorium in downtown Windsor, but before we had entered into a contract, the pastor from the Pentecostal church happened to be in a meeting in Detroit, and Francis told him that they were coming to Windsor in a couple of months, and he made his church available for the meetings that lasted three days. The meetings were fantastic, and many people received healings and miracles. I remember a particular incident where two of my friends were believing to be set free from cigarettes. One of them confessed that when he would be prayed for, he would be delivered, and that's exactly what happened. The other fellow said that maybe he would be delivered, and even thought he was prayed for, he did not get delivered. Interesting, eh? Our girls were 10 and 12 at that time, and at one meal, Charles and Francis took all of us out for lunch—the girls were ecstatic!

RETREAT CENTRE ON THE MOUNTAIN IN JAMACIA

While we were in Montego Bay, some interesting things happened. We rented a small car with stick shift. We had read in a Christian magazine about a Christian retreat centre up in the mountains near Montego Bay. So we went to the Bible bookstore and enquired about the retreat centre. The saleslady said, "Ask the two ladies behind you about it as they go nearly every week to the prayer meeting there." So we volunteered to take them to the centre if they would show us the way. We picked them up at their home and went to the meeting. When the meeting was finished, we got into the car and backed up, but none of the forward gears would work, except the high-speed gear, and then after a while, it didn't work. We were going down the mountain, so we coasted most of the way, but we knew that there was a small hill that we had to go over on the way down. Consequently, we kept the speed up and just made it over the small hill. When we finally stopped at the bottom of the mountain, we were able to get the high-speed gear to work, and then we drove to where the ladies lived, and they jumped out of the car as we slowly went past their house. Then we continued on down the highway to our motel, and then all gears stopped. Another exciting adventure!

HEALING OF ARTHRITIS IN THE BODY

We had been trained to pray for the sick. When we talked earlier about a retreat in a trailer camp, we left our seventeen-foot trailer there and eventually purchased a site and set it up with the hookups. A few years later, we came up for the long weekend in July, and our neighbours in the next trailer came over and explained that his wife, Hilma, had arthritis in her body; her hands were twisted, etc. We said to them, "We want to come over to your trailer tonight and pray for Hilma." They said no, but we insisted and came over to their trailer. I said, "Let me have your Bible. We want to read many of the scriptures on healing to you." They handed me a Bible, but it was in German. I could have gone back to our trailer and got my Bible, but the Holy Spirit gave me an idea. So I said, "I will give you the scripture reference, and you look it up in your German Bible, and tell us what you think it says in English." We did this for an hour, and then we prayed for her. There was no manifestation of any healing. We said good night and left.

Early the next morning, I got up, and as was my custom, I began walking to the washroom to shave and clean up. As I went past their trailer, the husband, whose name is Joe, came running out and said to me, "She slept all night without waking." I said, "Is that not normal?" And he said, "She is usually up several times during the night with the pain." The Holy Spirit on the inside of me said, "As this day proceeds, she will be healed, and at the end of the day, she will be able to walk faster than him." We were gone all day, and when we returned late in the afternoon, they came out of their trailer, and she beat him in getting to us. She was completely healed and no pain and no twisted hands. We rejoiced with them, and I felt I should tell them that sometimes the devil will try to put symptoms on you, but simply rebuke them if that happens.

The next holiday weekend in August, we were back, and they were there and said, "We have a story to tell you." It was wonderful when they got home, and Hilma could do all the things that she wanted to do. Then one day, all the symptoms returned, and Hilma called Joe and told him what had happened. We had given them a mini book on healing with many of the scriptures on healing in the back of it. Joe said, "Where is that mini book?" After getting it, they sat at the kitchen table, and Joe read all the scriptures three times, and then he took his fist and banged the table and commanded the devil to leave her, and all symptoms left for good. Fabulous, eh?

Chapter 4

More Yet

GOD LEADS US TO THIS FARM TRACTOR

Every farm needs a tractor. We were having a neighbour come and work up some of the fields for us. I had been looking around for a tractor and one Saturday, the Holy Spirit said to me, "This is the day you buy your tractor." He said, "Start in Leamington, and work your way towards Amherstburg, along Lake Erie shoreline." There was nothing in Leamington that I was looking for, and nothing in Harrow, but when I got to Kingsville, there was a shining John Deere tractor, the size I was looking for. I enquired about this tractor. The dealer told me that a farmer had bought it, and his son drove it when there was little coolant in the radiator and damaged the tractor. The farmer had it rebuilt and painted. He couldn't understand why it sat in his lot for months and nobody was interested in it. I believe God had that tractor there for me and nobody could buy it. I was! I explained that I lived on a farm near Owen Sound and if I bought it, how would I get it there. He said he was planning in the next week or two to take his mother in his pickup to the Owen Sound area. So I bought it, and he delivered it, and I paid half the cost of his gas and put him and his mother up for the night in the retreat centre. That tractor did me for twenty years.

GOD ANSWERED OUR PRAYER FOR A BIGGER FARM TRACTOR

Six years ago, I realized it was time to trade it in and get a bigger one, especially to pull the orchard sprayer that held 3,000 pounds of water. I prayed about it. Months passed, and nothing. So I asked the Holy Spirit what was wrong, and He told me that I had not detailed exactly what I wanted in this bigger tractor. So I said I wanted a tractor with 50 horsepower, a cab, heater and air conditioning, loader on the front, and a snowplow for the front and with 4×4. A few months later, the Holy Spirit said to me, "Your tractor has arrived." And I said, "Where is it?" He said, "In the town of Meaford." I said, "There is no John Deere dealer there, so it must be a Kubota tractor." The Holy Spirit said, "Yes, go see it tomorrow." I was there at exactly 8:00 a.m. when it opened. A salesman took me around the yard and showed me all the used tractors. They were all big tractors. He said, "That is it." I thought to myself, "I know I heard the Holy Spirit. What is wrong?" As I was walking out of their yard, there was a Kubota tractor parked at the back of the plant, so I yelled over to the salesman and asked, "Is this tractor in for repair or for resale?" He said, "Oh, I forgot. It just came in yesterday on a trade-in." It was exactly to the specs I had given the Lord, and it even had a snowblower for the front of the tractor. It was then cleaned up and tuned up, and I purchased it.

LARGER DISC

I had the need to get a larger disc. The one I had was old and was about six feet wide, and I needed one that was twelve feet wide. The Kubota dealer had one in their yard on consignment and had not been able to sell it. The problem was I didn't have the funds to buy it. I enquired who owned it, and it was a farmer I had previously sold garlic to. I contacted him and made an arrangement with him that I would do his farm tax return for the next year, and that's how I paid for the disc. It was not digging into the ground as it should, so

I had a fellow farmer look at it, and he explained that each section of the discs were installed incorrectly. In other words, the disc unit on the left side should be on the right side, and he helped me move them around. Then it dug properly into the ground. Thank you, Lord, for good neighbour farmers.

CARROT DIGGER

We were growing beautiful carrots but were breaking many of them off as we tried to dig them out of the ground. I prayed about it, and the Holy Spirit gave me a picture of a carrot digger. So I took an old cultivator and had a fellow take off all the cultivator parts that dug into the ground and rebuilt just one piece that went ten to twelve inches into the ground with a piece of flat bar sticking out the side at the bottom so that when you drove the tractor next to the row of carrots, this cultivator part went underneath the row of carrots and moved the ground and the carrot up so it was like milking a cow—you simply just pulled the carrots up and out of the ground. It worked fine. Thank you again, Holy Spirit.

RENTING A SMALL SCOOTER

My wife, Bonnie, and I want to give thanks to the Lord as our two daughters paid our way to spend four days in Niagara region and covered all our expenses as a gift on our fiftieth wedding anniversary. One of the mornings, we rented a small scooter each and buzzed around Niagara-on-the Lake and down the trails along the Niagara River. I was interesting that fifty years before that, we went to Bermuda on our honeymoon and had rented bikes with motors on them. If you were going up a hill, you had to pedal it to help out. We really enjoyed ourselves.

WHAT IT'S LIKE TO WALK WITH THE HOLY SPIRIT

HOW GOD SOLD OUR HOUSE IN WINDSOR

Years ago, we lived in Windsor on Norman Road. Bonnie's and my desire was to eventually live in the country. We put our home up for sale through a real estate company. We had several open houses, but no one made an offer. Time was moving on, and our prayers were getting more serious. On a Sunday morning, a car drove up into the driveway, with three people in it. The Holy Spirit said to me, "This is a real estate salesperson and a couple who will buy your house." They knocked at the door and explained that although there was an open house in the afternoon, could they walk through the house now. I said yes, and for the next hour, I walked them through the house explaining in detail all the improvements we had made. They said thank you and left. About supper time, we received a call from that real estate salesperson saying the couple was interested in the house, but the price was way too high. Knowing that they would buy it, I said we only have $1,000 to reduce the price by. He said, "Thank you, but it is not enough." Later in the evening we received a call saying the parents of the lady wanted to come and see it, and we said OK. They walked through it and also the greenhouse that we had in the backyard. The salesperson tried to get a few more thousand dollars of reduction, and we stood firm and said, "That's the lowest we are prepared to go." They agreed, and we called our real estate lady, and she prepared the papers, etc. That's what I call the Holy Spirit moving on our behalf.

PURCHASE OF A HOME IN THE COUNTRY

We were house hunting in the country and could find nothing that we liked. So after praying about it, we were led to take a piece of paper and write down exactly what we wanted. We were interested to having two rooms for an office and work area with a separate entrance. We gave the write-up to the real estate agent, and within days, she said that she had the perfect house and property for us. We were sceptical but went to see it. To our surprise, it met all the requirements that we wanted. We prayed about what we should offer, and the Lord gave us a price somewhat lower than they were asking. We presented the offer, and they accepted it.

CUTTING DEAD ELM TREE

There was a small woods next to this house, and in it was a dead elm tree. It was quite tall and near the electrical wires that went down the road. It leaned somewhat to the north, away from the electrical wires, and I carefully put the cut in the tree and began to cut through it. All of a sudden, it moved a little, but not the way I had planned, but towards the power lines, and if it fell down, it would knock down the power lines. What do I do? I went and sat down and prayed and said, "God, I have a problem. Can you send an angel and move the tree away from the power lines?" All of a sudden, I heard a large crash, and I knew that the tree had fallen down. I ran to it, and to my surprise and joy, it was moved and fell in the area where we had planned it to fall. Thank you, Lord!

FALLING ON CEMENT STAIRS

I shared earlier about the purchase of the farm near Owen Sound. There was a back entrance to the basement down cement stairs. During one winter, I had to go down these stairs to the basement, and unknown to me, there was a little ice on the top stair, and I slipped on it, and my back fell on the cement stairs with immense pain. As I lay there, I could see myself in a hospital bed with all kinds of support for my back. I said, "Lord, you know that I have a lot of things to do for you, and I cannot be laid up. So I ask you to heal my back." Instantly all the pain left, and there was no injury to my back. What a healing Jesus we have!

JESUS APPEARED IN THE FARMHOUSE

Within a couple of years after we purchased the farm, we turned the large farmhouse into a retreat centre with seven bedrooms and the ability to sleep twenty-three people. It had two showers, two washrooms, a large living room for meetings, and a good sized-country kitchen. Several years ago there was a group from Windsor. One day the group decided to go to town, but the pastor stayed back, and he was lying in his bed reading the Word. He heard footsteps coming up the stairs and someone walking down the hall. He figured that his wife had forgotten something and was coming into their room to pick it up. To his surprise, in walked Jesus with a white robe on, pulled up a chair, and sat down. He said to the pastor, "I wish to talk to you. Your life I see in three time zones." The first was the past and his ministry during that time, then the now time of what he was presently doing, and then the future that God had for him. The talk took about one hour, and the pastor was elated. I have often said I know that Jesus knows where the farmhouse is because He has been there. I have never seen Him in person—I look forward to that time.

UNDERSTANDING BETTER TO HEAR THE VOICE OF GOD

A few years ago, our family attended a Christian camp in Michigan. One of the teachings was on how to receive divine direction from God. This was in the early days when I was just learning to hear His voice. When the teaching was finished, I spoke to the speaker and said, "I didn't understand what you were saying." He then explained to me that God is like a radio tower that transmits a radio broadcast, and in order to receive it, we must have our radio plugged in and tuned into the proper station. He further explained that so it is with hearing God; you must be plugged into God (having a personal relationship with God) and tuned into God (spend time in his Word and with Him). That made sense to me. At this camp there was a man-made lake. I walked out on a floating dock. When

I reached the end of the dock, I looked down in the water and saw my reflection in the water. The witness of the Spirit came all over me, and the thought came to me, "If you will remain close to Me, the waves of interference will pass away, and you will clearly hear my voice and direction." Boy, was I excited. I now understood. I believe God has a sense of humour, because I was about to have to apply this in real life.

THE MISSING MONEY

As the camp was being closed, I volunteered to count the offerings for them. I prepared a cash count, listing the number of bills and the total. When I completed the task, the conference leader directed me to put the cash in a cigar box. Shortly afterwards, the cigar box was missing. Later, the cigar box was found on the conference leader's car seat. No one had remembered putting it there. I suggested we recount it. I found five 20-dollar and one 10-dollar bills missing. The conference leader said to me, "Let's pray and ask God who took it and where the $110 is." As we prayed, I saw a picture in my mind, but passed it off as ridiculous. The leader asked if I received anything, and I said no. The leader commented that the Lord told her that a young man, who I will call Mike, had taken the money. We confronted Mike, but he continually denied it. All of a sudden, I found myself saying to Mike, "In your right-hand back pocket, there are five 20-dollar and one 10-dollar bills." Dumbfounded, he reached in his pocket and threw the exact amount of bills on the floor, saying, "How did you know?" I had seen a picture of his blue jean pocket when we prayed. Because God gave me this information, I was able to minister to this boy and help him. A good example of the Holy Spirit working!

WHAT IT'S LIKE TO WALK WITH THE HOLY SPIRIT

SMUGGLING CHRISTIAN BOOKS INTO CUBA TWENTY-FIVE YEARS AGO

Have you ever been instructed by the Holy Spirit to take a trip into a communist country and take in a large quantity of Christian books? I would guess, about twenty-five years ago, the Holy Spirit said to me, "I want you and Bonnie to go to Cuba and bring with you ten copies of every teaching book that Kenneth Hagin has printed in Spanish." Do you have any idea how many books that is? Well, first of all, I have to ask Bonnie to be in agreement and go to Cuba with me. Initially, she said, "You're crazy." So I said, "You pray about it." She did and came back and said, "The Holy Spirit said we were to go." So I ordered the books—there were about 100 pounds of books. I contacted a ministry that smuggled Bibles into Russia and other communist countries, and they told me how to pack them inside blue jeans, shirts, and keep them in the bottom of suitcase and clothes on top, etc. We booked the flight for two weeks in the winter. We borrowed four really large suitcases and packed everything into them. In those days, you were allowed two suitcases each and heavier weight.

The time came to go. We flew out of Toronto to Cuba. I sat next to a fellow in the plane, and he told me this was his seventh time in Cuba. He said he really liked Cuba, except for one thing. I asked him what that was, and he said the strict customs inspection. He said they take everything out of your suitcase and check it and you put it back in. The sweat formed on my forehead and ran down my face. I said to the Lord, "You told us to go, and I believe with all my heart that you will take care of us."

When we landed, the suitcases were hauled into the terminal and just laid out on the floor. People dug through them, picked up theirs, and headed for the inspection tables. We could only find three of our suitcases, and we waited until everyone had picked up theirs and went into inspection area. As the inspection area was thinning out, I spotted our fourth suitcase in the inspection area. So I said to Bonnie, "You take one, and I'll take two." And we went to the inspection area. In those days, the custom people were dressed in army uniforms, and each carried a gun—to me they all looked like Castro, with their beards.

When we arrived there, one of the inspectors said to me, "Is this your suitcase?" I said, "Yes, we have been looking all over for it." So he said, "Then you two come with me." We went into another room, walked through it, and then another room, and we were now outside the building, and there was a bus (much like our Greyhound buses with places on the side to put the luggage). The customs officer took each suitcase and stowed it in the place for luggage and then looked at us, smiled, and said, "You two, have a great time in Cuba." So we were the only people on the plane that did not get their luggage inspected.

The day after we arrived at the motel, we rented a Russian car. Now we had asked the ministry that took Bibles into Russia, etc., what to do with our books, and they gave us a map on how to get to an underground church. You must remember that in those days, Bibles and Christian books were forbidden in Cuba and anyone found with them were jailed, and many pastors were never heard of again. We had cut the map into four parts and put each part in a pocket in the blue jeans in each suitcase. We also brought Crayons, toothbrushes, toothpaste, extra blue jeans, etc., with us. So we put the map together and drove for about two hours to this old run-down church building that was supposedly closed. There was no one there. What do we do now? There was a house not far away, and the thought went through me, "That's the home of the pastor." But I had to be sure. So I walked up to the house. There was no door on it, but rather a sheet of cloth, and I knocked on the frame of the entrance. A lady appeared, and immediately the anointing of the Lord came all over me, and I knew it was OK to try and talk to her. She knew very little English, but she understood the word "Christian" and invited us in. We then showed her some of the Christian books, and she had us hide the rental car behind the church, and we carried the four suitcases into her house. She contacted one other person, we presume, to advise her husband and others that Christians from Canada were there with Spanish teaching books.

Within minutes, about twenty people arrived. One person knew a little English, and he translated for us. We formed a large circle, and we sang worship songs to them, and they sang the same songs in Spanish to the same tune. There were tears all over the place. The pastor, later on, told me that there were just enough teaching books so that everyone in his church received one book for that week, and they were to bring them back and exchange for another book the next week. He figured there was enough teaching material for one year for his entire church. As an afterthought, he saw an apple in our car and said they had not eaten one for years. So the next day, we returned with a large bag of organic apples that we had grown and taken with us to Cuba. One man invited us to follow him to his farm and gave us a tour. We began to realize that each farm grew different things, and I noticed that they ate only what they obtained from other members of their church. This fellow said to us, "My house is your house." And we understood that we could come anytime and visit them. How nice of them! And shall I say how nice of God to arrange for us to clear customs and be a part of blessing these wonderful Cuban Christians. This, of course, was the highlight of our vacation in Cuba!

CHAPTER 5

Moving on in the Holy Spirit

HOW GOD BROUGHT US TO THE HOUSE TO RENT

Now as the time neared for us to move out of our home and move up near the farm, we began to look in the Owen Sound newspaper for possible rentals in the country near the farm—there were none. Obviously, there were all kinds of rentals in Owen Sound and some in the village of Chatsworth, but we wanted to be near the farm. We knew that it was not God's plan for us to live in the farmhouse as it was a retreat ordained of God. The Bible talks about the benefit of fervent prayer, and we did that as we could not find a place to rent. Then the Holy Spirit said to us, "The next time you go up to the farm, I will show you the house to rent." We were excited! So we went up on a Thursday, got the newspaper, but no rentals. Friday was the same and also for Saturday. We were going home on Sunday—what gives. So we asked the Holy Spirit what to do, and He instructed us the go visit a dear friend of ours nearby. We visited him right away and asked if he knew of any rentals in the area. He said no. Then he said, "You know, there is a home next to us that is empty. It was purchased by a fellow from Germany, and he works for the US military in purchasing. Why don't you contact the real estate firm that listed it and make contact with him in Germany." The real estate lady did that and explained that we were looking for a rental for a year or two. He replied that he was interested and set a date in two weeks to meet us at the house. He flew out, and we met at the house. We loved it, and the rental was good, and we were to cut the grass and take care of the place. So a few weeks later, we moved up to this house and moved in.

FINDING THE PROPERTY TO BUILD OUR HOUSE

While we lived there in the rental house, we looked around to try and find a reliable contractor to build us a house. Our plan was to build the house in our vineyard, but there was a problem. The vineyard was in the middle of the Niagara Escarpment Plan, and they had a condition that personal homes could not be built there. We appealed their decision, and a hearing was set in their office in Georgetown. We made our appeal, and although they were sympathetic, they turned down our appeal. As you can understand, we were greatly disappointed. We then turned to the Lord in prayer and said, "God, what do we do?" The Holy Spirit said there was a lot for sale nearby and had been for sale for five years—each year they reduced the price. There would be an old sign along the fence beside the road. So we went to the neighbour, and she couldn't think of anything. After a while, she said, "Wait a minute, there was a lot on the Massie Road east of where your farm is." We drove along the Massie Road and found the old sign and contacted the real estate lady. She said the property was two acres and was still for sale. She related the price, that it went on the market five years ago and how it dropped each year in price. It was now the middle of winter, and we didn't know if the property had large stones on it or not. We were encouraged by the Holy Spirit to walk on the property. The moment we began to walk on the property, the anointing of God fell on us with an assurance to proceed. We purchased the property.

HOW GOD DIRECTED US TO HAVE OUR HOME BUILT

Now, we had to find a contractor to build the house. So we prayed about it. The Holy Spirit said to us, "Go to the yellow pages under 'modular homes.'" We did, and there were three firms that built them. So I said, "OK, Lord, I'll get a price from all three." The Holy Spirit said, "No, only deal with Quality Homes." So I called them and said, "Why would I buy a house built in a factory?" They said, "Please come and look at our models. We have plans for fifty-plus homes that we could build for you."

So we went and were impressed. They said to us, "Our management wants to get a good backlog of work this spring, so we are offering everyone only for this month $7,000 off the purchase price and throwing in all the seven appliances." So we got serious fast and found one plan that we really liked on one level with a full basement. Various changes could be made to it in their computer, so we had several things changed and purchased the house. They dug the hole and put in the cement foundation and footings. We were responsible for the driveway, the septic system, the well and the trench for the hydro and telephone lines. The house was built in one week in their plant and delivered the following Monday morning on four transports with a large crane. Each section was lifted and moved into place, and in the next two days, the drywall was fixed between the sections along with the shingles, etc. In a couple of weeks, the brick was put on. They gave us a ten-year warranty on everything in the house. We had a few minor problems, and they came and fixed them. The house is now fourteen years old. I understand that they never offered those kind of discounts again, only that one year. We again thank God for directing us on the purchase of our home.

NEW LAMINATED WOOD FLOOR

A few years ago, we wanted to replace the rugs in a part of our home with laminated wood. A friend of ours called up and said there was a sale on, three boxes for the price of two, which works out to a discount of 33%. We got samples and found one that suited us. We had the dimensions of what we needed. We went to purchase the material. The manager of the store waited on us. When he entered the purchase in the machine, it keep giving him a discount of 50%

and not 33%. Only for us it worked out to 50%; he couldn't understand it and got so frustrated that he said to us, "I don't understand, but that's your price." So we got the material at a discount of 50%.

FAMILY ROOM BUILT

In the basement where we planned on building the family room, it was just the bare walls and joists on the ceiling. We talked to a brother in the Lord who did renovations, and he said, "My wife and I will do the work for no charge if you pay for the material." That's what we did and ended up with a beautiful family room.

THE DOG THAT GOD HAD FOR US

A number of years ago, we prayed about getting a dog for the farm, one that could catch ground hogs but still be a friendly dog. Bonnie spoke with a fellow worker at Walmart who was moving and had to give her farm dog to someone. Bonnie invited her to come to the farm on the weekend, and she and her husband came out in a pickup. When they arrived, this dog of theirs jumped out of the back of the pickup and ran up to me and began lapping my face. It was a border collie with half of his face white and half black. We took him, and I believe that first year, he killed twenty-three ground hogs. I remember the first time he saw a ground hog; he danced around it and then by instinct grabbed it in the middle of its body and shook it till it was dead. Amazing how instinct leads dogs. I can remember also the first time he encountered a skunk and got his nose right up under his tail and got it in the mouth and nose. Remarkably, his instinct took over, and he went and rubbed his face in the ground and grass, and within one hour all smell was gone. He never got near a skunk again. We got him when he was three years old and had him eleven years before his death.

HOW GOD HAD WINDOWS REPLACED

The farmhouse had nineteen windows, and they were the old single type, and much heat was lost in the winter. We were thinking of replacing two of the windows and were talking to a brother in the Lord about it. He said, "Why don't you measure all the windows and get a price to replace them." It didn't make sense, but we did it anyways. Home Depot gave us a price of between $7,000 and $8,000 as they were different sizes. A friend of mine knew the owner of a Mennonite glass plant, and we were able to get a price for these windows. They were all triple glazed, with all windows having screens, and windows could be removed, and it came with a lifetime guarantee. Their price was $4,000. When I passed on the pricing to this fellow, he said, "I am sending you a cheque for $4,000. Go ahead and order them." Another friend of ours installed them free of charge for us. Praise the Lord.

HOW GOD GOT THE RUGS INSTALLED

Shortly after we had ordered the windows, another brother in the Lord who installed rugs for Home Depot said he could get half a dozen rugs in excellent shape as someone wanted their three-year-old rugs removed and new ones put in. This brother also installed them for us at no cost. Another praise to the Lord! I should add that the day he was bringing us the rugs, it was very icy, and there is a large hill you have to climb to get to our home, and with his van, he ran off the road. He called CAA who came out but couldn't help him, and then a second CAA truck came, and it could not help him. Then an old truck came slowly over the top of the hill and stopped beside them and asked if they needed help. They said yes, and the fellow in the old truck attached a chain to their van and pulled it out with the old truck (it was not a 4×4, just an old truck with rear drive). Once he unhooked the chain, he and the truck disappeared. This had to be an angel driving an old truck.

HOW AN ANGEL FIXED THE DRIVE BELT IN A CAR

Speaking of angels, I remember a retreat that was at the farmhouse, and on the participants' way home, the drive belt in their van broke. It was a Sunday afternoon, and what should they do? So they prayed. In the distance they say a man walking towards them in a short-sleeved shirt. I mention that because it was the middle of winter. He looked at the problem and said, "Hold on, I can get you what you need. I'll be right back." Before long, he returned with the right belt and installed it. Then when they went to thank him, he disappeared! Another angel, I believe!

VACATION ARRANGED BY GOD

Shortly after we purchased the farm, the Lord said to me, "If I were to bring you $7,000 for a vacation, would you spend it on vacation?" I said, "I only need about $2,000 to $3,000 for a vacation." There was no response from the Lord, so I said, "Do you really want me to spend $7,000 on a vacation?" And He said yes. So I said OK. Weeks later I received a letter in the mail advising me that I had won $7,000 in the April in Aruba contest. Whoa!

VACATION IN ARUBA

We planned on going to Aruba in early January, and I tried to get accommodations in a less expensive hotel, but it was booked solid. So I prayed about it, and when I awoke the next morning, the Lord said to me, "Concord, Concord, Concord." I didn't know initially what that meant, but then I remembered reading in a book on Aruba about a new hotel, and it was called Concord. So I said, "Lord, is that where you want us to book?" He said yes. We booked it—it was the most expensive hotel on the island. When we were there, we would meet couples on the beach and agree to have dinner together. The meals were expensive, about $50 each. In nearly all the cases, the couples were one Jewish and one Gentile. And in every case, there was always an opportunity to share what Jesus had done in our lives. So we spent the $7,000, and evangelized to many people and had a glorious vacation.

VACATION IN MAUI

A few years before our vacation in Aruba, the Lord requested us to go to the island of Maui for vacation and that I was to spend three days and two nights on top of the mountain there. You are able to drive to the top of the mountain at 10,000 feet and hike down to the 7,000-foot level where the crater is. The crater is several miles wide and looks just like the surface of the moon. I had read about it on a previous trip. You enter a draw with your name, and only one person wins—there are normally fifty to one hundred people who enter for each night. I won for the first night, but not the second night. I enquired of the Lord, and He said there would be a cancellation and to call them ahead of time and say I wanted it.

MOUNTAINTOP EXPERIENCE

After we arrived in Maui, I called the office on top of the mountain and explained that I had the first night but asked them to save me the second night if someone cancelled. They told me no one ever cancels. So starting four days before my trip, I called every day, and they kept saying no one cancelled. But the day before I was to leave, when I called, they said, "I can't believe it, there is a cancellation, and you can have the second night." So I was ready for my three days and two nights on the crater. The other cabin was across the crater on the other side. I had to rest often, as you know the air at that altitude is very thin. There was of course no hydro, and the cooking was on a wood stove. The highlight of the trip was the second night. Earlier in the day I read the account in the Bible about how Daniel had prayed and it took twenty-one days for the angel to get through and it was the archangel Michael. The Lord said to me, "Thus it shall be tonight." That meant to me that an angel would visit me. So as it got dark, I put out two candles, set my chair to look at the door, and put another chair on the other side of the table. I sat there and waited for it to get dark. It got real dark, but no angel. I began praying in the Holy Spirit (tongues), and I began seeing things. It was something that happened to a one-year-old baby, then something else to a two-year-old child, then a three-year-old child, then a four-year-old child, and then I recognized it was me. I saw pictures as I grew up and through my teens, and then my twenties until I got married to Bonnie. Then there were things that happened in our married life, and then the Holy Spirit said that I had the choice in my later years of five different options. After I had the five options explained, I asked the Lord what was his preference, and He said number 5, and I said, "OK, I want number 5." This still has not happened yet at the date of writing this book. After it was all over, the Holy Spirit showed me an angel speaking into my ear all these things. So an angel did come, but I was not allowed to see it.

HOW GOD SAVED A HOUSE FROM BURNING DOWN

A few years ago when we lived just outside of Windsor in the country, I was invited to speak at a church near Amherstburg. I talked on hearing the voice of the Lord. There was a lady there with a small baby. Several times she had to leave the room with the baby. I remember thinking to myself, how much of this teaching did she absorb? Well, within a week I found out. She lived in the country with her husband and five children. It was a Thursday night, and at about 2:00 a.m. the baby woke up, and she fed the baby. After that, she lay down in bed to go back to sleep, but the Spirit of the Lord kept saying to her in a gentle voice, "Go downstairs." At first she didn't pay any attention to it, but then she thought about what the fellow on Sunday morning said, that if the Lord directs you to do something, do it right away. So she got up and went downstairs, and to her surprise, the front porch was on fire. She called the fire department and got her family out of the house before the smoke filled the whole house. She called me and said that if she had not listened and did what the Holy Spirit said to her, they would have all perished. She reiterated to me, "Keep telling people to instantly obey the Holy Spirit." Thank you, Lord.

DELIVERED OF SMOKING

I mentioned earlier that I worked for a material handling company in Windsor. The purchasing manager reported to me. He smoked continually, and his office was always full of smoke. I said to him one day, "Have you ever thought about quitting this smoking?" He said definitively, "I have tried just about everything and no help." So I said, "May I pray for you?" And with his concurrence, I did. I was away the next day (Friday) and returned the following Tuesday. I was no more than one minute in my office than he walked in and said, "I have a fantastic story to tell you." On the next day after praying for him, he would normally have a smoke before his shower, then another smoke before breakfast, and then another on the way to work. He said, when he got up, there was no desire to smoke, and he didn't smoke before he got to work. He set the package of cigarettes on his desk and looked at them all day and never touched them. God set him free—then he came to the Lord, and then his wife and then his two boys. The way to go, Lord.

DISCERNMENT WORKING

I worked for this company for nineteen years. Somewhere about year 15, I had this experience. It was the first working day in the new year. One of the managers came to me and said, "I want to be friends with you." For some reason we were always at odds, even in the general manager's meetings. I found this very odd, and I felt a warning in my spirit. I went to our office manager and alerted him to watch out for anything not right that had to do with this fellow. Within a week, the office manager came to me and reported that one of the ironworkers in the installation crew was asking about his payroll, and when they looked together at the payroll sheet, this fellow said, "It shows that I received pay for two weeks in January, but I didn't work those weeks." It was reported to me, and we made arrangements with the bank to get the cancelled cheques to date from the bank. On the back of the cheque was a signature, but it was not the ironworker's signature. Then there was another signature after that of this manager. We then checked the previous two months, and they were all OK. So it only started in January. I showed it all to the general manager, and then we contacted the detective branch of the city police department. They verified everything and made copies, etc. They suggested we set up a trap for him, but somehow he got wind of it and resigned. The company proceeded to make charges against him for the recovery of the money. This was a result of God's discernment that he gave to me.

CHAPTER 6

The Holy Spirit in Action

SEWER LINE WORD OF KNOWLEDGE

Earlier I talked about living on Norman Road in Windsor. One summer the sewage line got plugged up, and I believe it was the result of roots on trees getting into it. We tried everything to get it free, but to no avail. I had a Christian brother in the Lord that was quite sensitive to the Holy Spirit. I asked him to come over and see what he gets. He walked around for a while, and then he said to me, "There is a blockage right here in the front lawn. I will get my son-in-law and come back tomorrow and dig it out." The next day they dug down about eight or nine feet and found the sewage line. He said to me, "It is right here." So we broke the line, and the sewage water filled up the hole, and then to our surprise, the water all ran away. We climbed down in the hole and found an old sewage line that began there, so we hooked up the two lines together, and it worked fine. The Holy Spirit had shown this fellow exactly where the problem was and what to do. I love being part of what the Holy Spirit is doing.

GOD DIRECTED ME TO PURCHASE THE HONDA FOR MY WIFE

Just before we moved up north to the Owen Sound area, we needed to replace Bonnie's old car. I said to the Lord I am not mechanical and would not know if a used car was in good shape or not. So I asked the Lord to show me the car and I would buy it. A couple of weeks went by, and then one day the Lord said to me, "What are you doing?" And I said, "Resting." He said, "This is the day you buy Bonnie a car." So I took her car and drove to the end of the driveway and then said, "Which way, Lord, because to the right is Essex and to the left is Windsor." He said, "To Windsor." Then in what I call a stern voice, the Lord said to me, "I don't want you ever again buying Bonnie a domestic car." I was surprised and asked what I should get her, and the Lord said a Honda or Toyota. So I went to the Toyota dealership and asked them what they had in three-year-old Corollas. They had only one, and the salesman had it for the day. So I then went to the Honda dealership. There were three Honda Civics, and I tried all three. I knew in my spirit which one the Lord wanted Bonnie to have—it was silver in colour and low mileage. I asked the salesman, if he would be on duty that evening as I was going to bring my wife in to look at the three cars. He said yes, and I said, "I will see you tonight."

I went home and said to Bonnie that I had a surprise for her and asked her to go with me to Windsor that evening. She said yes and asked me what it was for, but I wouldn't tell her. So after supper, we drove to Windsor, and I pointed out the three cars. She immediately said, "That silver one is to be my car." I still had her drive all three, but she really liked the silver one. The salesman had informed me earlier that there is not the markup on foreign cars that there is on domestic cars. We got the price they were asking for the Civic.

I prayed about it, and I still felt we should make an offer $1,000 less than their asking price. The salesman said it was too low and we would not get it at that price. I said, "Then we will look someplace else tomorrow." He was gone for a long time to speak with the sales manager. The sales manager and the salesman came back and said to me, "You have come in with a very low offer to purchase. Let me ask you something. As tomorrow is the last day of July and we have had a very good month of sales in July, could you come up with the money tomorrow? If you can, then we would accept your offer, but if not, we can only drop the price by $500." I said, "Yes, we can get the money tomorrow." Then I said, "Help, Lord." The Holy Spirit said to me, "Go to the bank in the town of Essex tomorrow at exactly 9:00 a.m." So I did just that, and as I pulled into the parking lot, the manager also drove in. So upon asking, he invited me to come into the bank, and I explained the whole thing to him and also that our house was closing soon and we had sufficient to cover the cost. He took copies of everything and said, "I will try to get approval, but it may not happen today." He called me in the early afternoon and said, "The loan money is in your account." We were able to write a cheque to the car dealer that day and get the car. Hallelujah! God is good!

A RACING MIND HEALED

Sometime ago, I spoke at a Full Gospel Business Men's meeting in Kincardine, Ontario. I shared how I got saved, filled with the Holy Spirit, and how God had moved on my behalf and blessed me. After my testimony, I usually move in the gifts of the Holy Spirit. I sensed the Holy Spirit saying to me that there was someone there that was involved in a car accident and had had several operations since then. Also that there was still one thing that has not been healed. A lady came up to the front and said that fit her perfectly and that she had one thing left that had not been healed. She explained that she had a racing mind and even when she went to bed, her mind would not stop thinking of this and that.

After I prayed for her and she was slain in the spirit, she tried to get up, but she was unable. After an hour, she motioned to my wife that she was getting cold on the floor and would she get her coat and help her on with it. After another hour, she couldn't get up, and as the meeting was ending, some men lifted her up and took her to her husband's car. She was really under the power of God. I got her telephone number and phoned her a few days later, and she explained that when she woke up the next morning, the racing mind was gone and she was free. Thank you, Jesus!

APPENDICITIS ATTACK AND DEAL WITH GOD

One of our daughters on two occasions had an appendicitis attack, and I took her to the hospital. She was about six years old at the time. The first time with medication, it subsided. The second time she was kept overnight, and it was explained to us that they might have to operate the next day. While she was kept in bed, she said to the Lord, "I will make a deal with you. If you heal me, I will read my Bible every day." She was completely healed and sent home. She never again had appendicitis problems, and she read her Bible daily. I tell people to stand on the promises and don't try to make deals with God. In hindsight, I can only surmise that God knew her heart and honoured it.

BOOK OF F. F. BOSWORTH

Have you ever done something that the Holy Spirit told you to do and it impacted your life? Bonnie and I flew to an island off of Mexico called Cozumel, and the minute I stepped off the plane, the Holy Spirit said to me, "You have a book in your suitcase by F. F. Bosworth, and I want you this week to read it and highlight the important things in it." When I got home, I typed out the highlighted areas, and the Holy Spirit told me to read it one hundred times, which I did. It helped me to believe in faith for healing for me and others.

GOD GOT US A PICKUP FREE

Over the last few years, we have been believing for a pickup truck for the farm. Just recently, we received a call from a previous client in my accounting practice. He enquired whether I was interested in getting a pickup from him. I said, interested, "Well, we have been praying about a pickup for years, and yes, we are interested." He explained that his company's insurance costs had risen sharply and that it would cost him $3,000 a year for the pickup, and as he hardly used it anymore, he was thinking of selling it as it was in good shape. So he decided to ask the Holy Spirit if he should sell it, and the Holy Spirit said to him, "No, give it to Norm Weber." I asked him how much he wanted for it, and he said, "No cost—it's yours." We agreed to meet halfway between Windsor and Owen Sound in London, so we met him there and had lunch. He also obtained a safety certificate and had the necessary work done at his cost. He also gave me $360 cash and said, "You will need this to pay for the transfer tax and new licence. It is a Ford F150 pickup and silver in colour." We drove it home and praised the Lord.

GOD ARRANGED FOR HYDRO BILL OF TWO YEARS TO BE PAID FOR

About the same time as we got the pickup truck, we received twenty-seven envelopes from Hydro One (our hydro supplier) with a month's billing in each one. At this time, there were thousands of people that had not received a billing for their hydro costs for the last two or more years, and we were one of them. This pertained to our farm. We had been chasing them for months trying to get the billings. It was for $3,975, and upon checking, we found out they had left out six payments, and there were other errors. We obtained proof of our payments from the bank and mailed it to them. They put through an adjustment for the amount of the payments but would not admit they made an error. This reduced the balance owing to about $2,900. As we didn't have that amount available, we prayed to the Lord about it. My wife, Bonnie, was speaking to a friend of ours in London about it. This lady called back in a couple of days and said she had a friend who would help us out on the billing. She asked for the account number with Hydro One, and we supplied it to her. I thought even if they paid $500 on it, it would help a lot. We found out the next week that this friend of hers paid $3,000 on the account, and it was paid off—praise the Lord!

THE 99.9% LOVE OFFER

From time to time, I think all of us think back on the time we courted someone special that eventually became your mate. Bonnie and I had been dating for about six months, and we found ourselves beginning to fall in love with each other. Up until this time, I had been what they call a late bloomer—I was not ready for marriage. If a girl I was dating began talking about marriage, I ended the relationship. I had been brought up by my parents to be honest in all things. So when I thought about telling Bonnie I loved her, it meant to me that I wanted to marry her, spend my life with her, raise children together, etc. I was not completely ready for that yet, so what I did was to tell Bonnie I loved her 99.9%. At first it didn't seem to matter, but as the weeks and months went by, it became an irritable situation with Bonnie. She thought, "He loves me, or he doesn't?" She was seriously thinking of breaking off the relationship. Then there came that time when I could truly say with all my heart that I loved her 100% and wanted to marry her and spend my life with her. Then we got engaged and began planning our wedding and our life together.

DAUGHTER SAVED FROM DROWNING

I was thinking the other day about the time our youngest daughter, Cheryl, nearly drowned in the lake. We had visited some friends who had a cottage on Lake Erie. Cheryl was two years old at the time and was playing at the edge of the water. I was watching her, and all of a sudden she stood up and took a step or two into the water and went under. I ran into the water and grabbed her, and she was crying as she had gotten frightened. It really shook me up. If I had not been watching her, she could have easily drowned. Praise God, I saw her in time and was able to rescue her.

IMPACTED TOOTH

In 1999 we moved from the Windsor, Ontario, area to Owen Sound, Ontario, which is about five hours driving in a north-east direction. We rented a house for about a year and a half. Normally I visit the dentist to have my teeth cleaned and checked about once every year. So I found a dentist that was recommended and made an appointment. As I was a new client to him, he x-rayed all my teeth. Then he explained to me that I had an impacted tooth that was very high up in my mouth and the top of it touched the bottom of the opening for my nose. So I said, "Don't worry about it, just leave it alone." He said, "You don't understand. It has a cavity in it and should be removed soon." He sent me to a specialist in Kitchener who explained more fully to me the procedure and its risks. They would do surgery into the gum and remove the tooth, but there was the risk that there would be an opening thereafter from my nose to my mouth. The skin would be sown over the incision, but sometimes it didn't work. I did not like that. The date of the procedure was set in a few months. I asked the Lord how I should pray for that, and He gave me two scriptures—Mark 11, verses 23 and 24. Let me show you what it says from the Amplified Bible, "Truly I tell you, whoever says to this mountain, be lifted up and thrown into the sea, and does not doubt at all in his heart, but believes that what he says will take place, it will be done for him. For this reason I am telling you, whatever you ask for in prayer, believe—trust and be confident—that it is granted to you, and you will [get it]."

IMPACTED TOOTH MOVED DOWN BY THE HOLY SPIRIT

My confession was that the impacted tooth would move down and there would be no risk of an opening. I decided to quote those two scriptures many times every day as it related to the impacted tooth. The Friday before the Tuesday of the surgery, I arranged for an x-ray to be taken, and it showed the impacted tooth had not moved.

Now, in the next day or two, this area of my mouth felt tender as if something was happening under the gum. The specialist in Kitchener was a Jewish man. They gave me a gas that made me half asleep, with that "don't care" attitude. When the surgery was complete and the impacted tooth removed, the dentist looked me right in the face and stated, "I don't know what happened, but that impacted tooth had somehow moved down." And there was no risk of an opening into my nose. I said to him, "That's my God and your God." And he smiled. So in essence, that impacted tooth moved down in my mouth a couple of days before the surgery and after I had that x-ray done. Just in case you didn't know, my God and your God can move teeth in your mouth if you believe!

LOST DAUGHTERS FOUND AT DUSK IN THE WOODS

Several years ago, when our daughters were teenagers, we went to a lodge in the Muskoka district during the Christmas season. We had wanted to do a lot of cross-country skiing, but there was little or no snow. So we spent hours walking in the paths in the bush. One day the four of us decided to go for a long walk on the paths, but as the boots of one of the girls leaked, only Bonnie and I went on the walk. When we came back, we gave Bonnie's boots to one daughter, and then they decided to go for a walk themselves and follow our tracks. We had crossed a large flat rock, but when they got there, they picked up another set of tracks that went across the top of the lake. It was now getting into late afternoon, and they continued following the tracks, and it got dark. We realized that something was wrong as they didn't return, and we explained this to the owner. He took his snowmobile and followed their tracts and realized that they were going the wrong way. So he came back and said, "If they keep on going the way they are going, they will come out on a road." So we all hopped into the car and drove there, and a young girl flagged down our car and asked how to get back to the lodge. We said, "Hop in," and of course they saw us in the car. They were quite relieved to see us. It was scary to think that they could have spent the whole night in the woods if we had not found them. Praise God for his leading.

CHILDREN FILLED WITH THE HOLY SPIRIT AND SPEAKING IN TONGUES

Back in the seventies, Bonnie and I got filled with the Holy Spirit and received our tongues. Our two daughters kept bugging us about praying for them to receive the gift. One was four and the other six. We thought them to be too young. But they kept after us to pray for them, and we did. When we prayed for each of them, one of them saw a coloured ball flying around in the room and then went directly into her stomach area. We often say the Holy Spirit dwells in the stomach area. The Bible says that out of your innermost being shall flow rivers of living water, and we say it flows out of our stomach area. Interesting, eh?

TRANSPORT MISSED US

Each of us has experienced construction delays on highways. One day we were stopped on Highway 401, and I looked up in my mirror, and I saw a transport come barrelling down the highway towards me, and then I realized he wasn't going to be able to stop before reaching us, and there was nothing we could do but pray. Just before he reached us, he pulled the transport off the pavement and flew past us on the shoulder and eventually stopped. Thank you, Lord, for protecting us!

CHAPTER 7

More of the Holy Spirit

ANGEL APPEARED AT DAUGHTER'S WEDDING

Many years ago, when we lived in the country outside of Windsor, Ontario, our eldest daughter was married in a service in our backyard—it was large and about one acre in size. Following the service, the wedding party went to a famous garden in Windsor to get pictures taken. A lady walked up to my daughter and said, "You are the most beautiful bride in this park." And when my daughter turned quickly to tell her new husband, the lady disappeared—even if she had run, we would have seen her. We concluded that she was an angel.

VISION FOR GREENHOUSE

During the first year of our married life, we went out to Western Canada on vacation. We travelled throughout British Columbia and over to Vancouver Island. We visited the world-famous Butchart Gardens, and I said to Bonnie, "When we get home, I am going to build a small greenhouse in the backyard." When we got home, I forgot all about it, but my wife reminded me and said how much I would enjoy it. We heard of someone who had a greenhouse in their backyard, and it was just the size I was looking for—about twenty feet long and six feet wide. I ordered the uprights from a lumber company made out of cedar wood and planed at the top for the glass to fit, and erected it. I was able to get the glass at a good price. By the end of the year, it was complete and painted. On January 1, I dug up many flowers that were still blooming and transplanted them into the greenhouse. The next day, the it froze as it snowed. Those flowers bloomed for weeks in the greenhouse. Don't you think that sometimes it is a good idea to listen to your wife!

SWEARING CLIENT SWEARS NO MORE

I had an accounting client that swore continually. One day he came to me and said that in a few weeks he was going to Hungary. "What must I do before I leave to take care of things in case of an accident or something?" I said, "Get a will made out, talk to your family about what they should do if you don't return. And thirdly, you need to pray and ask God to forgive your sins, and invite Jesus into your heart as Lord and Saviour." I helped him do this. After he returned from Hungary weeks later, I was simply amazed—he did not swear anymore. The Holy Spirit dealt with him in this area of his life. Who says God doesn't work in your life if you accept Him!

PASTOR HEALED OF COLD IN SERVICE

For many years, we attended a Pentecostal church. One Sunday, our pastor could hardly talk because of a cold. When he was trying to speak, my wife and I walked up to the front and prayed for him. He was instantly healed. We had followed the leading of the Holy Spirit.

BACK HEALED

We are friends with an evangelist named Gene Lilly from Orlando, Florida. We had him speaking to a group of people in our home. After he spoke, he invited people to come forward for prayer.

A very large man, probably weighing 275 pounds, said he had bad back pain. Some of the people prayed for fell under the power to the floor; sometimes we call it slain in the Holy Spirit. We usually have a person stand behind them, just in case. This fellow braced himself and said he was not going down. The evangelist prayed for him, and he went down. While he was lying on the floor, his legs began to move out and in by the power of the Holy Spirit. He kept complaining, "Who is pulling my legs?" as he couldn't see his legs. No one was pulling his legs, but rather the Holy Spirit. When it finally stopped moving, he was helped up, and all the pain was gone.

ACCOUNTING CLIENT HEALED IN THE OFFICE

I ran an accounting office in my home, and a certain client would come from time to time to discuss a business situation. Then he would say, "Do you have a minute to pray for this or that problem?" In many cases, he was slain in the spirit and, in most cases, healed. In hindsight, I think for prayer first and created an excuse to talk about his business. Even today, years after I retired from accounting, he calls to discuss business and then asks for prayer over the phone and, in most cases, is healed.

UNUSUAL WORD OF KNOWLEDGE

Sometime ago, I spoke in Oshawa, Ontario, and shared my testimony and ministered under the power of the Holy Spirit. I received a word of knowledge from the Holy Spirit that someone there had five holes in them and I was to pray for them. I didn't know what it meant, but I spoke it out anyways. A well-built fellow came forward immediately and said to me, "That's me." He shared that he was a police officer in New Brunswick and got shot five times and lived. He was still having problems with the holes in his body not healing well. I prayed for him, and I understand that the holes were completely healed.

CHRISTMAS BOOK GIFTS

I worked for a materials handling company in Windsor for nineteen years. Each Christmas season, I purchased Christian books and wrapped them and gave them to about twenty people. They often kidded me and said, "Don't waste your money as I'll just throw it in the garbage." The amazing thing was that several of them, over the years, would come to my office and say, "Can I talk to you for a minute?" And I would shut my office door and listen. In many cases I prayed for them for their problems or concern. Interesting, isn't it?

ENCOURAGEMENT TO A LADY

I spoke at a Full Gospel Business Men's Meeting in Parry Sound, Ontario. The Holy Spirit told me that there was a woman going to be there who invited new people to her home for lunch and fellowship after the service. Some of these people were rather rough.

Many people told her not to do it. The Holy Spirit told me to tell her that God was pleased with her and to continue doing as before. I asked the Holy Spirit how I could identify her, and the Holy Spirit said she had her arm in a sling and that I would have no problem identifying her. Sure enough, a lady came in with her arm in a sling, and upon talking with her, she admitted that she was the one who invited people to come to her home after church. I encouraged her and said God was pleased with her.

SPEAKING PROPHETICALLY

Another time, I was asked to speak at a community centre in Colpoys Bay, Ontario. It was to be a Saturday night meeting, and on the Thursday before the Saturday, the Holy Spirit spoke to me that I was to prophetically speak to every person in the meeting. I was dumbfounded. I prayed and prayed about that, and continually got confirmation that it was what the Holy Spirit wanted me to do.

Before the meeting started, I spoke to the leadership of this meeting and explained what I was going to do. They were excited! I found out that the Holy Spirit had instructed them to pray for me to do exactly that!

There were about twenty-five people there, and I spoke prophetically into each one. I would call them up to the front and then ask the Holy Spirit what I was to say, and within a couple of minutes, a distinct thought came into my spirit, and I spoke it out. There were many tears and comments that no one knew about the particular situation I spoke of. Obviously, the Holy Spirit knew, and people were ministered to!

RELEASING A PERSON THROUGH FORGIVENESS THAT BROUGHT HEALING

It's amazing how you can be sitting in a meeting with not a care in the world and the Holy Spirit speaks to you to do something. That happened to me, and the Holy Spirit said that a certain person that was sitting in the back of the church had intense pain in their body, and He wanted me to get him free. I went to the back of the church and sat down beside this particular fellow. I said, "I believe you are in intense pain." he said, "Yes, all through my body." I then asked the Holy Spirit why, and He said it was because of unforgiveness towards his wife, whom I knew was playing around with other men. I said to him, "You have a choice to make, either put up with the pain or make a quality decision to forgive your wife." He looked at me and said, "I want to be rid of the pain." So I said, "You pray and forgive your wife." And he did, and within five minutes all the pain left.

THROUGH CONFESSION OF FORGIVENESS, MANY PEOPLE ARE HEALED

Unforgiveness can affect you badly if you allow it to grow. Years ago, I brought a speaker to a meeting in Detroit, and he taught on the power of forgiveness, and then he said, "I want each of you to search your heart, and if you have any unforgiveness, make a quality decision to forgive that person, and when you do, there is going to be a healing that will take place in your body, and when that happens, I want you to stand up." During the next five minutes, nothing happened—it seemed like half an hour as I sat there and sweated. The devil kept trying to say to me, "No one is going to stand up." I rebuked that thought and prayed for a manifestation of the Holy Spirit's power. Then one person stood up and then another and another, and before long, nearly half the people there stood up with surprised looks on their faces and smiles. It's amazing what unforgiveness can do.

GOD KEPT THE CAR GOING FOR HOURS AFTER GAS RAN OUT

As mentioned earlier in another chapter, our family vacationed on the island of Maui in the Pacific. We decided to make an all-day trip around the island and follow the map. This would be from one side of the island around the top and then down part of the other side and then straight across back home. On the map, it showed at the top of the island dotted lines, which would mean to me a gravel or dirt road, but still a road, and it connected with the regular paved roads. We were halfway through the day and now entering the gravel road. We had not seen a gas station for a couple of hours and were getting low on gas. Thinking that there would be one shortly, we continued on. The so-called road got rougher and rougher, and many times there were sheep or other animals grazing on the road. At times the road was exceptionally narrow, and in some cases, the edge of the road dropped several hundred feet. Our gas gage went to zero, and we prayed and continued on for hours after that. We were reminded by the Lord of that story in the Bible where the oil was multiplied. In the evening we came to the far side of the island where the road was paved. Incidentally, we talked to some of the natives, who said it had been years since a car came by. Gas stations were closed, and we made it back to the motel. We estimated that we had driven five to six hours on an empty tank. Hey, God knows how to put gas in a tank supernaturally—we thank Him for it.

WORD OF KNOWLEDGE WORKING

We were invited to a small town in Texas called Winnie. We told people later that this is the town where Winnie the Pooh came from (kidding, of course). Anyways, I was teaching on hearing the voice of the Lord, and when I started having words of knowledge about people with certain problems, it went on and on, and we had to get their leaders to pray with these people as there were so many people coming up. They just ran up, got healed, and ran back to their seats. I've never seen anything like that before.

STARTING A NEW CHAPTER OF FULL GOSPEL BUSINESS MEN'S FELLOWSHIP

One day, the Holy Spirit said to me, "I want you to go to Lion's Head and start a new chapter of Full Gospel Business Men's Fellowship." I didn't know where this town was, but after studying a map, I found it, and it was about one hour and a half north of where I lived. I made up a flyer and had the post office put it into everyone's mailbox. I knew a pastor in the area and met with him. The Holy Spirit instructed me to meet the pastor on a certain day, and I did. Then he said to me, "There is a luncheon today noon at a lodge, and several other pastors will be there. Would you like to come along?" And I said, "Definitely, yes." I had the opportunity to speak to the group, and they said they would advertise the upcoming meeting in their churches. They did, and about eight people attended the first introductory meeting. We then met every two weeks and talked and prayed and eventually started a new chapter that is still in operation today, years later.

FORGIVENESS FREES A LADY

A few years ago, my son-in-law received a contract to work in Australia for one year in designing computer programs, and he and his family went there. Our two daughters put together their aeroplane miles and paid for my wife and me to fly to and from Australia for one month. I had an opportunity to speak at a meeting of the Full Gospel Business Men's Fellowship, and the Holy Spirit gave me a word about someone who held unforgiveness in their heart and I was not to proceed on until this was resolved. The daughter of the president of Full Gospel in Australia was there and reluctantly admitted that it was her and then forgave her dad. The father was elated and was thankful to God that a problem in their family was resolved. As a result of this, I had the opportunity to meet privately with their president and share ideas, and I later on presented some of these ideas to the board of directors in Canada.

TEACHING ON HOW TO HEAL THE SICK

My wife and I were invited to teach and speak at a church in Edmonton, Alberta, on the subject of how to heal the sick to a class and have them practice on one another. It started on a Friday night and Saturday morning and afternoon. Normally we take eight to ten weeks to teach it, but we covered all the material. I then spoke at the church service on Sunday morning, and following that, the newly trained people prayed for those that needed prayer, and a new, what I call, altar worker team members were birthed in that church.

LARGE TUMOUR DISAPPEARED

From time to time in our church in Owen Sound, we would pray for people at the front of the church. This one Sunday, we were up at the front praying, and as it was finishing, a lady said to my wife, "I want you to meet my sister who has a large tumour sticking from her stomach." After the introductions, my wife laid her hand on the tumour, cursed it, and commanded it to shrink and be gone, and that was a quick prayer. Well, that lady was scheduled for surgery the next Friday, and even though it had completely shrunk, the doctors did surgery and could not even find enough tissue to get a sample to test. I think back on a lot of prayers that Jesus said, and they were always short. Long prayers sound great, but in many cases the short ones work too.

SEVENTY-SIX-PAGE MANUAL BIRTHED

Over the years we gained a lot of knowledge and experience in flowing in the Holy Spirit and being led by the Spirit of God. When we were living in the Windsor, Ontario, area, we approached our pastor and said we would be prepared to train altar workers to minister and pray at the front of the church. He agreed, and we started our first class there. We had about twenty people. As the years went by, we trained more classes so that eventually we had about fifty people trained. Our pastor encouraged us to write a manual on how to get people healed. I knew it would take a lot of time to write it up, and I kept delaying doing it. Eventually, the Holy Spirit spoke to me and instructed me to get up every morning one hour earlier and begin writing. It took me a year to write up the manual, which has several chapters and covers seventy-six pages. (My wife checked it for spelling and ensured that all the Bible references were correct.) We have taught it in many cities and churches. Generally, we find as we teach it and practice on one another that people get healed.

CHAPTER 8

Moving Further in the Holy Spirit

DIRECTIONS OF THE HOLY SPIRIT REGARDING THE FARM

A few days after we purchased the farm, the Holy Spirit directed me to take a folding chair and my Bible and go and sit in the middle of a field of oats and barley. It seemed a strange thing to do, but I have learned to do what I hear. After I sat down, the Holy Spirit directed me to read Psalm 1. This chapter is only six verses long. I read it and reread again and again. In essence it says blessed, happy, fortunate, prosperous, and enviable is the man who does not waste his time listening to the advice of the worldly, but meditates, ponders, and studies the Word and follows the direction of the Holy Spirit.

You and I run into many people who have all kinds of advice and comments on things. The Lord was saying, "Only listen to Me and check out things with Me." The Holy Spirit went on to say that as God had provided the funds to pay for the farm, then it was His. So I said, "You want the farm registered as belonging to the Father, Son, and Holy Spirit." He said, "No, but register it in both your names and that every major decision affecting the farm must be approved by Me." To start with, He gave me three conditions to follow. First is that the farm is never to be put up as security for a loan or mortgage; second, we are never to live there permanently, such as retirement; and third, the farm is to be used to minister to His people and for the growing of organic food as directed. As the years went by, we have followed those directions. For the first several years, the Holy Spirit would direct us what major project we were to do that year, such as building a root cellar, building a water ram system, planting the orchards, working up fields to grow food in, purchasing a tractor and equipment, etc. As the farmhouse was converted into a retreat centre, many people have been blessed and ministered to, and it keeps on going today.

MEDITATE THE WORD LIKE SHEEP CHEW THEIR CUD

One day before we had the vineyard, the upper field was a hay field, and we had rented out several fields and the barn to a neighbour who had sheep on the farm. It was most interesting during the winter months as the little ones were being born in the barn. On a summer day the Holy Spirit directed me to again take a folding chair and go sit in this field next to the road and watch. The sheep were there, and they were eating grass. Then as if by command, they all sat down and continued to chew. After a while, I realized that they were like cows that chewed their cud and that they had more than one stomach. It was at this moment that the Holy Spirit said to me, "Start chewing the Word. Take a scripture, read and reread, check references—mediate the Word." I began to do this.

MY POWER IS THE SAME HERE AS IN THE PHILIPPINES

We had the privilege of going to the Philippines in the Pacific for a week. They are a beautiful people. Getting there was another thing. We flew from Toronto to Los Angeles, then to Manila, and then a local plane to Davao City. This local plane stunk—the people took on board pigs, goats, chickens, ducks, etc. It was quite an experience. The whole trip took close to twenty-four hours. The first day after we arrived, we were invited to be part of a ministry team praying for people. The evangelist spoke in English and was translated into the Philippine language. We were told not to try and figure out what they wanted prayer for, but rather to pray for them for healing in the name of Jesus. By the end of the ministry time, I was simply amazed—there was a pile of crutches, braces, etc., that people no longer needed as they were healed. I was upset with the Lord as this took place in the Philippines and not in Canada or the USA. When I had some quiet time with the Holy Spirit, I asked this question. To my surprise, the Lord said to me, "My power is the same here as in your home country. They simply believed My Word." What a revelation that was to me. When I returned home, I could hardly wait to tell people about the healings. They would say, "That's nice," and then talk about something else. I was shocked. You would be too. Now I understood—these people could not afford to pay for a doctor or go to a hospital—their only hope was to believe the promises in the Word.

MAXIMUM BONUS

I shared earlier in another chapter how I worked for a local manufacturing company in Windsor and how they were bought out when the original owner retired. The first full year under their new direction, the company showed a profit. Prior to the year end of the company, a profit-sharing plan was worked out and approved for those in supervision. I was one of them, and because I was the VP of finance, my share would be larger than most. The plan called for many calculations to arrive at the total to be shared. It also had a limit built into it. As it worked out, once all the calculations were made and confirmed, it turned out that it just reached the maximum that could be paid. I was asked several times if I had adjusted something in the financial statements to have it work out to the maximum, and I said definitely no. I would never do that. Even a year later, I had a few enquiries from the new owners about it. To tell you the truth, I was surprised it figured out to the maximum allowed. I enquired of the Lord about it one day, and the Holy Spirit informed me that God planned it so that certain people that belonged to Him would get the most they could, and of course all the rest of the supervision got blessed because of it.

Some people may have a problem with that, but I believe it!

GETTING YOUR NEEDS MET

Being a member of Full Gospel Business Men's Fellowship in Canada and being a leader there, I attended yearly an advance, or as some people call it, a retreat. It generally took place on a weekend in early June at Trent University in Peterborough, Ontario. I really enjoy these, and one year, the Lord began to speak to me about three levels of prosperity that I needed to understand and teach. Let me share briefly these three levels. Level 1 is what I call "getting your needs met." It is based on Luke 6:38, which says, "Give, and it shall be given unto you; good measure, pressed down, and shaken together, and running over, shall men give unto your bosom. For with the same measure that ye mete withal it shall be measured to you again." This is quite a promise, for it says that as we give, it shall be given back to us in an overflowing manner, good measure, pressed down, shaken together, and running over. I go for that; wouldn't you? Obviously, we must believe it and call it in. So if we do that and believe it, we get our needs met.

WALKING IN ABUNDANCE

Level 2 is what I call "walking in abundance." It is based on 2 Corinthians 9:6–8 in the Amplified Version, which says, "(Remember) this: he who sows sparingly and grudgingly will also reap sparingly and grudgingly, and he who sows generously and that blessings may come to someone, will also reap generously and with blessings. Let each one (give) as he has made up his own mind and purposed in his heart, not reluctantly or sorrowfully or under compulsion, for God loves (that is, He takes pleasure in, prizes above other things, and is unwilling to abandon or to do without) a cheerful (joyous, prompt-

ver—whose heart is in his giving. And God is able to
grace (every favour and earthly blessing) come to you in
ce, so that you may always and under all circumstances and
er the need, be self-sufficient possessing enough to require no
aid or support and furnished in abundance for every good work and
charitable donation."

I have heard people say, "I don't need abundance, just my needs met." But wouldn't you like to be a part of God's army, blessing others? I do. Recapping, it says as we sow generously and cheerfully, God promises in His Word to bless us abundantly so that we have the funds to bless others (every good work and charitable donation). Can you really believe it? If so, stand on that Word and call it in.

FINANCING THE GOSPEL

Level 3 I call "financing the Gospel." You've heard of superstores, super churches, etc. Well, God has a further or higher level of super abundance. Let me share two scriptures that verify that. The first is Ecclesiastes 2:26 (Amplified Version), which says, "For to the person that pleases Him, God gives wisdom, knowledge and joy; but to the sinner He gives the work of gathering and heaping up, that he may give to one, who pleases God." And the other scripture is from Proverbs 13:22 (second half), which says, "And the wealth of the sinner (finds its way eventually) into the hands of the righteous, for whom it was laid up."

PAYMASTER OF THE LORD

So what that says to me is that the job of the sinner is to gather and heap up and to transfer into the hands of you, the righteous. Do you think the sinners have done a good job in gathering up? I think you would say yes. While we are on the subject, let me tell you what the Holy Spirit has said to me regarding how to receive it. First is to develop your faith and believe the promises in God's Word, second is to ask God to send forth angels to bring into your hands, and third is to tell God you will not just spend it on yourself, but invest it, only as God directs. Do you know what the Holy Spirit told me? That He then calls them a "paymaster of the Lord." How would you like to become one of them?

DELIVERED FROM A CURSE

Several years ago when we lived just outside of Windsor, one of our friends got quite ill and ended up in the hospital, but they were unable to help him and sent him home. He had that grayish look, as if he were approaching death. Many people, including us, had prayed for him. At this time I had my accounting office in my home, and it was during tax time. The wife of this fellow came to our home to pick up my wife and go to the Women's Aglow meeting. She stuck her head into my office and said hello. At that precise moment, the Holy Spirit said to me, "Call you wife and pray together in a circle, and I will tell you what is wrong with her husband." The lady thought I was nuts, but we all held hands and asked the Lord to reveal to us why he was so sick. The Lord spoke to me and said that it was a curse and that after the Women's Aglow meeting, we were to follow this woman home and lay hands on her husband and rebuke the curse. Well, that's what we did. I asked her husband then if I could pray for him, and he said, "Definitely yes." I broke the curse off him, and within minutes the colour on his face changed, and within hours he was completely normal. Thank you, Lord, for your word of knowledge!

AUDIBLE VOICE OF THE LORD DIRECTING

Earlier we shared how we went to Aruba on vacation, and while there, we spent a whole day with the Lord and asked for direction as I was going out on my own in doing accounting work and auditing. We did not receive direction from the Lord that day. We had arrived home from Aruba on a Saturday and went to church on Sunday. The pastor preached on 1 Samuel 3:4–10, which talked about the audible voice of the Lord. God called out loud to Samuel, saying, "Samuel." Samuel thought it was Eli calling him, and Eli said it wasn't. Again God called, "Samuel," and Eli said it was not him. Eli realized that it was the Lord, so he told Samuel that if his name was called again, say, "Speak, Lord, for thy servant heareth." And God spoke to Samuel.

The next day, Monday, I had all my work planned out. First of all, I went out to the backyard to check the greenhouse and heard my name being called out loud, "Norman, Norman." There had been times when my wife had called me for a telephone call, but she always called me Norm. I went into the house and said, "Did you call me?" She said no, and immediately we both knew it was the Lord. I went to my office and began praying in the Spirit. A thought or, rather, an instruction would come to me. It would become stronger and stronger until I wrote it down, and then the thought immediately left. This happened five times. The resulting messages were explicit direction for the start of my new business. This has been the only time in my life to date that I have heard the audible voice of the Lord.

SHARING THE GOSPEL WITH CANCER CENTRE DRIVERS

In February of 2014, I was diagnosed as having prostate cancer. I was given a needle in the stomach that prevented the cancer from spreading and arranged to start radiation at the cancer centre in Kitchener, about two hours away. The arrangement with the Canadian Cancer Society was that you pay them $100 up front and they arrange for volunteers to transport you from your home to the cancer centre and back and forth to where you stay during the week and home on weekends for the seven and half weeks of treatment. This began in September and finished in early November. I experienced some degree of tiredness, but none of the other side effects. The experience has been that with the thirty-nine treatments over seven and a half weeks, the cancer is eliminated in the prostate. Praise the Lord! During these weeks of treatment, there were various drivers that drove me to the cancer centre. I had the privilege of being able to share the gospel with every one of these drivers. Many had never heard about being born again and inviting Jesus into their heart as Lord and Saviour.

TITHING

We hear a lot today about tithing to the Lord where you are fed, such as your church. In 1975 the truth of this matter became real to Bonnie and me. We began tithing that year. When I totalled up everything at the end of the year, I discovered that I had not paid fully the 10% tithe. After that I kept a running log of my income and tithes paid so that I would not miss it. The Bible is full of promises when you tithe, and undoubtedly you have read many of the blessings in this book as we tithed.

SALE OF TRAILER

I mentioned earlier that following a retreat in a trailer camp and meeting in the upper part of a barn, we decided to buy a lot there and place our trailer on it. It was a seventeen-foot trailer, and we had just finished purchasing a much larger one. So we put the seventeen-foot trailer up for sale. A couple came by to look at the trailer, and the Lord said to me they are going to buy it. As you know, people try to get the price reduced, but as I knew they were going to buy it, I did not reduce the price, and they paid what we had asked for it. Thank you, Lord.

HIT BY A CAR

When I was two years old, I ran out into the street and was hit by a car and was unconscious. The milkman was there at the time and took me to the hospital, and I recovered fully. My parents kept reminding me to look both ways before crossing the street. When I was 5, I again walked out on the road and immediately thought about what my parents said, and when I was halfway across the street and looked, a car was coming, and I froze and got hit again. I can still remember it to this day. Again I was taken to the hospital and recovered. Thank you, Jesus, for protecting me.

PROTECTION FROM A FALLING TREE

I remember cutting dead trees in the woods. I felled a dead elm tree, and as the tree went down away from me, a huge piece broke off and came right at me, and I froze. The piece of wood was Y shaped, and one part was on one side of me and the other part on the other side, and I didn't get hurt at all. Another thank you, Jesus, for protecting me.

THE TILTED BIN OF APPLES

There is one other story that I could have been badly hurt. There is a section of the apple orchard that slopes quite a bit, and there was a bin of apples there. I drove in with the farm tractor with the forks on the front of the tractor, and when I lifted up the bin of apples, the tractor began to tip sideways. I never had that happen before, and instantly without thinking, I dropped the bin of apples on the ground, and the tractor righted itself, and I was spared an accident. Again, that you, Lord.

MY WIFE'S VISIT TO HEAVEN

One last story I want to share with you. When my wife, Bonnie, was about eleven years old, she had a bad case of the red measles. She came down with an appendicitis attack. It was so bad she was throwing up bile. Because she had the red measles, they would not allow her to come to the hospital in Chatham. So her mother phoned a doctor that she knew in London, and he said to get her in an ambulance and get her to London. It was in the middle of the winter and a very bad snowstorm. It took twice as long to make the trip because of the storm. During the trip, her appendicitis broke open, and the poison went into her body, and she died. When she died, she remembers going through a tunnel with a very bright white light at the end of it, and she arrived in heaven. Jesus talked to her and said, "Will you come now?" She said, "Yes." And He said to her, "What about your mother, whom you are living with?" And she said, "You have taken care of my mother and me since my father died. You will take care of her." Jesus said, "I have work for you to do—you must go back." So she went back down the tunnel and could see the ambulance slowing, making its way down the highway, and she went through the roof of the ambulance and into her mouth and into her body. She of course was a spirit. When they arrived at the hospital, the doctor asked her how was the pain, and she said there was no pain. They then realized it must have broken open and rushed her to surgery and operated on her. The amazing thing was that she had received a bad bruise when someone ran into her skating and it had formed a large sack, and most of the poison was in the sack. So she lived. Praise the Lord.

SUMMARY

As mentioned at the very beginning of this book, the Holy Spirit instructed me to write testimonies that my wife and I lived. There are about a hundred testimonies in this book. We trust that they are an inspiration to you.

I have always said, if God can do it for me, He can do it for you. God bless.

CHAPTER 9

Praying for New Body Parts

Praying for new body parts is foreign to most Christians. It was to me also, until the summer of 2014 when I sensed the Holy Spirit saying to me to pray to God for me to come up to the third heaven, where God is located. I did that, and in the Spirit I found myself in a large room like a library, and I was directed by an angel to climb up the stairs (which were made of gold, and the handrail was gold also). At the top of the landing was a sliding door like you see in a barn, a large door that opened, and I was led by an angel (I knew the angel was with me, but I could not see the angel) into the body parts warehouse, which was the biggest building I have ever been in. It must have been miles long and wide. In it were rows of body parts hanging under a sign that showed the person's name. We walked for a long time, and I could see everything was alphabetical, and eventually I knew I was to look up, and there on a plaque was my proper name, Norman William Weber, and date of birth. All kinds of body parts were hanging there, kidneys, heart, prostate gland, arteries and veins, liver, joints, bones, nerves, ligaments, tendons, etc. I then had the understanding that we could claim them by faith for people that needed them.

Body Part Miracle no1 a year and a half went by, and in January 2016, I received a call from a friend in Windsor who had a very bad knee, where the bones were rubbing together and extremely painful. I had learned at this point to ask the Lord how to pray for people and would, in most cases, get a leading from the Lord. So I did that, and to my surprise, the Holy Spirit said to me to pray for new knee parts. I asked how and was instructed to pray for new ligaments and tendons and attach them to the knee, then for a new knee cap, and then for other parts of the knee, and then I was instructed to pray in the spirit (in tongues) for five to ten minutes until the Lord said it was done. I later sensed that this praying in the spirit was the time it took for an angel to install the body part. In fact, later on, I would get the percentage of installation done, such as 25% or 50%, etc. For this fellow, after about seven minutes, the Lord said it was done, and when I told him that, he said a few seconds before that all the pain left and everything worked like a new knee. He could walk and run with no pain. That became what I have called body part miracle no. 1.

Let me tell you about body part miracle no. 2. I received a call from a fellow who told me that his doctor said he had a damaged tendon going into his ankle and a damaged tendon going into his rump. I prayed for new tendons and then prayed in the Spirit for five to ten minutes. When I got the OK that it was finished or installed, all the pain left and never came back.

Body part miracle no. 3 was from a fellow who tripped when he stepped into a hole, possibly a ground hog hole, and tore a ligament and damaged the cushion in his knee. I prayed for a new ligament to be attached to replace the damaged one and a new cushion in the knee and then prayed in the Spirit for five to ten minutes. As I finished, the fellow said the pain was gone and he was able to walk and jump with that leg. Previously, he had walked with a limp, and when he showed up at the office the next day, people kept asking him what happened as he no longer walked with a limp. He hesitated, then said, "Well, I have a friend that prays for people for new body parts, and he prayed for me, and I received some new body parts, and now I can walk normally and with no pain." Some believed him, and some didn't, but they had to admit something good had happened.

Body part miracle no. 4. This was one of God's arrangements. My wife, Bonnie, had an appointment in town in the morning and one in the afternoon, so she took our car and dropped me off at our farm, which is two kilometres away from our home. I said I would come back home for lunch at noon and take the farm tractor. I always take the garage door opener or key with me, but somehow that day I did not (I personally think God had me forget them). Well, at lunch I hopped into the tractor and drove it home. As I pulled into our driveway, I thought, "Where is my garage door opener or key?" And I realized I had neither of them. The house was locked up, and I couldn't get in to eat lunch. I asked the Lord what to do, and he said to me to call a Christian neighbour and see if I could join them for lunch, which I did, and they invited me to come over. We had lunch together, and the man of the house shared that he had damaged nerves on the bottom of his feet. I offered to pray for new nerves on his feet and then pray in the Spirit for five to ten minutes. He agreed, and we did the prayers. At the end of the praying in the Spirit, all pain left, and he was able to walk normally with no pain. I have followed up on him, and he remains pain-free.

Body part miracle no. 5 is quite a story. A lady from our church came over to our home with her nine-year-old daughter who had hurt her knee, and it was painful to walk on it. On praying to the Lord for what to do, we sensed that the cushion in the knee was damaged. I explained to the girl that I could pray for a new cushion in the knee and then pray in the Spirit. She and her mother were in favour of doing that. After prayer, the pain left. An hour later, the pain returned, and I asked the Lord what it was all about. He said it was only the symptoms of pain and nothing was wrong with the new knee. So I rebuked the pain, and it left. Another hour later, it returned, and I explained to the girl that she had the authority to kick the symptoms of pain out of her knee. She then did that, and it left. Later on in the evening, the pain came back, and she said with authority, "Get out." And it left and never came back. The girl learned a lot from this exercise.

Body part miracle no. 6. A lady at church approached me and asked me to pray for the constant pain in her leg and foot. I asked the Lord about it, and He said it was damaged nerves. I did the same thing, prayed for new nerves in the leg and foot and prayed in the Spirit. In this case, because of the anointing at that prayer time, I only had to pray in the Spirit about two minutes and all pain was gone and new nerves were installed. Interesting, eh?

Body part miracle no. 7. A young lady that smoked like a chimney could hardly breathe because of the damage of smoking to her lungs. I explained to her that I could pray for a new set of lungs and that her agreement with this would be very important. She agree, and I did that and then prayed in the Spirit for a short time. Next day, her breathing was completely normal, and we thanked the Lord for the new set of lungs. I encouraged her to ask the Lord to help her give up smoking, and she said she would.

Body part miracle no. 8. One of my neighbours is a Christian and is retired from working in an auto plant in Windsor. As there was some air pollution over the years, this resulted to some damage to his lungs so that when he had a cold or flu, it would settle in his lungs and last for many weeks, sometimes months. We were talking recently that he was presently having a bad bout with infection in his lungs and considerable coughing. I explained to him how we pray for new body parts and then pray in tongues until the Lord says to stop. He asked me to pray for a new set of lungs, which I did, and then I prayed for about five minutes in tongues until the Lord said to me it was complete. Everything cleared up in hours, and he said it felt like he had a new lung, and he could now breathe normally, like he did as a young lad.

Body part miracle no. 9. We used to live in Windsor, Ontario. A previous accounting client of mine called me and in the discussion shared the pain he as having in his hip or pelvic area. After telling him about praying for new body parts, I volunteered to pray for him.

We prayed for a new hip and then prayed in tongues for five or six minutes. All pain left, and it felt to him like he had a brand-new hip.

Body part miracle no. 10. I had another telephone conversation with a fellow who had constant pain at the bottom of his spine. The doctor told him he had damage in the sacrum. So I prayed for a brand-new sacrum, which is the bone, I understand, at the bottom of his spine. Again I prayed in tongues for a short period of time, and as I told him it was now complete, he said the pain had just left.

Body part miracle no. 11. A dear friend of ours developed leukemia (cancer of the blood) a few years ago. We have prayed for him from time to time. Because of his condition, his spleen became enlarged over the months so that his stomach extended out about four to five inches, and he looked like he was a seven-month-pregnant woman. I shared what God was doing on new body parts and offered to pray for him. I prayed for him and then prayed in the Spirit until the Lord said to stop. A few days after I prayed for him, he called me and said the extension of four to five inches had shrunk down. About one month later, his doctor checked him over and was surprised to advise him that his spleen was the normal size. So in this case we had proof that the spleen was normal size by a doctor.

Body part miracle no. 12. A friend of ours visited us just recently, and in the conversation he shared how his knee had been rather painful the last couple of years. Also he stated that he had herniated discs in his back and that it was very painful, especially when he had to left heavy things in his work. We talked to him about praying for new body parts, and he was quite excited and asked us to pray for him. We (my wife, a lady friend, and I) prayed then for both problems and asked God to put in a new knee and a new spine. Then as usual we prayed in the Spirit until the Holy Spirit said it was completed. The next day he phoned me and was quite excited and said there was no pain either in his knee or his back. Praise the Lord!

Body part miracle no. 13. I had heard about a fellow in North Bay, Ontario, that had a dream, and in the dream he was taken to the body parts warehouse and saw all the body parts available for the body of Christ. I was able to find him and spoke to him. It was quite exciting to find someone else that had seen the body parts warehouse in the third heaven. He commented that his wife was soon to go through surgery on her knees as they were quite painful. I asked him to consider having myself pray for new knees for her. She was quite excited about this, and both the husband and the wife got on the phone with me, and we prayed for new knees for her and then prayed in the Spirit until released by the Holy Spirit. Immediately upon completion of praying in the Holy Spirit, the pain left, and she started dancing in their kitchen and was looking forward to sharing with the doctor what Dr. Jesus had done for her.

Body part miracle no. 14. A friend of mine whom I have known for twenty-five years or so and have not seen for some time visited us. He shared that he had a lot of pain in his back continually. I explained about the body parts ministry, and he was open to praying for him. I asked the Holy Spirit how to pray and what to pray. He told me to pray for a new spine and new nerves from the spine to various parts of his body. I did that and then prayed in tongues for about five minutes until the Lord said it was done and completely installed. I have talked to him since that time, and all pain is gone, and he is able to lift things without any pain at all.

Body part miracle no. 15. I received a call from a fellow in Windsor. We have many friends there, as we used to live there. He said, "This is embarrassing. If I am sitting down and go to get up, I would have to get to the bathroom in five seconds or I would wet myself." Also he had to go many times to the bathroom on the slightest urge to go there. He brought extra clothes to work as he would wet himself many times. He was the owner of a business. He said, "Norm, please pray for me." I said, "Give me a minute or two, and I will ask the Lord." I was thinking of praying for a new bladder, but the Holy Spirit said, "Just pray for new nerves that control the bladder." I did that and prayed in tongues, and next day he called me and said, "It is fantastic to be able to go to the washroom only a few times a day and no rush."

Body part miracle no. 16. My wife and I visited a lady who is a pedicurist and works on people's feet and toes. She shared how she had pain in the ball and socket joint in her right hip. We offered to pray for her and asked the Lord specifically how to pray for her. The Lord told us to pray for a new right hip, and we did that and again prayed in tongues until released by the Holy Spirit. She immediately felt a reduction in the pain. Over the next few minutes, the rest of the pain went away. She is one happy camper!

Body part miracle no. 17. I received a call from a friend of mine in another city. He is in his seventies, but he likes to exercise on a bike and go swimming. He normally goes on the bike for twenty-four minutes but reduced it to about seven minutes because of the pain. He had received new body parts earlier on another part of his body when I had prayed for him sometime ago. He called me and suggested I ask God what was wrong and what needed to be done. The pain was under his knee and up his left leg. The Lord said to me that his tendons and ligaments were wearing out, and when he rode the bike, it caused inflammation there. I said to the Lord that I could rebuke the inflammation, but the Lord said it would only come back again. I was instructed by the Lord to pray for new tendons and ligaments, which I did, and all pain left within ten minutes.

Body part miracle no. 18. A friend of mine told me that when he was a child, he had pneumonia, and over the years he had a tickling in his bronchial area, and it often got sore and infected. So I asked the Lord, "Do I pray for a new bronchial?" The answer was, "No. Pray for new linings of the bronchial and new linings in the tube that comes into the bronchial." I did that and then, as usual, prayed in the Spirit until the Holy Spirit said it was complete. All the previous tingling sensation left for good. Praise the Lord!

Body part miracle no. 19. Another friend of mine who is a Christian and believes in healing called and told me that he was working underneath his car and reached to one side with a large wrench and jerked too hard. What happened was that he tore a ligament going from under his arm across his chest. He said that he heard it snap. He suffered intense pain when he moved the arm on that side of his body. By the time I found out about this, he had suffered for two weeks. So here I prayed for a new ligament and then in tongues for several minutes, until the Holy Spirit said it was completely installed. Shortly thereafter, all pain went away, and he was able to move his arm in different ways with no pain. He attended the meetings of Full Gospel Business Men's and was one who never sang any of the songs we sang. The following meeting, I noticed that he was now singing with everyone else. He was an elated fellow.

Body part miracle no. 20. A couple that we knew several years ago came and visited us. It was nice having fellowship with them and getting caught up on everything. In the process, the lady excused herself for constantly clearing her throat. I asked her why she had to do that, and she explained that her thyroid gland was underactive, and although she took iodine supplements, the condition caused her to clear her throat quite often. So after explaining how the new body parts miracles worked, I prayed for a new thyroid gland, and within minutes, she stopped having to clear her throat.

Body part miracle no. 21. A friend of mine helped me put on the snowblower on my farm tractor. As it was mounted on the front of the tractor, and quite heavy, it was hard to get it into place to be properly attached. In the process, this fellow yanked it hard and hurt his shoulder. The next day he could not turn his head sideways or lift up his right arm. So I called him and explained that I could pray for a new shoulder for him and God would install it. He agreed, and I prayed for him and in tongues, and he received a new shoulder and then could move his head sideways and lift up his arm.

Body part miracle no. 22. Another friend of mine had a bad hernia. I asked the Lord how to pray for it and was instructed to pray for a new body part that held all the organs in place, which I did, and there was no hernia anymore.

Body part miracle no. 23. A fellow came to visit me recently and had a lot of pain in one knee. He is an avid fisherman, and this situation was interfering with his hobby. As is the practice, I prayed for him and then in tongues, and all pain left. He is enjoying his fishing now.

The Holy Spirit showed me at the beginning of 2016 that many of his believers are prematurely dying before their time, for many reasons such as poor life style, poor eating habits etc., and God has sent angels to specifically work with the body of Christ to install new body parts in his children where needed. This chapter illustrates in twenty-three real life testimonies how believers were prayed for and received new body parts in the year 2016.

PRAYER FOR SALVATION

Heavenly Father, I come to You in the Name of Jesus. Your word says, "Whosoever shall call on the name of the Lord shall be saved" (Acts 2:21). I am calling on You. I pray and ask Jesus to come into my heart and be Lord over my life according to Romans 10:9-10: "If thou shalt confess with thy mouth the Lord Jesus, and shalt believe in thine heart that God hath raised him from the dead, thou shalt be saved. For with the heart man believeth unto righteousness; and with the mouth confession is made unto salvation." I do that now. I confess that Jesus is Lord, and I believe in my heart that God raised Him from the dead. I AM NOW REBORN! I AM A CHRISTIAN—A CHILD OF ALMIGHTY GOD! I AM SAVED!

PRAYER FOR THE BAPTISM IN THE HOLY SPIRIT

Jesus, you also said in the Word: "If ye then, being evil, know how to give good gifts unto your children: HOW MUCH MORE shall your heavenly Father give the Holy Spirit to them that ask him?" (Luke 11:13). Say, Jesus fill me with the Holy Spirit and with the evidence of speaking in tongues. Holy Spirit, rise up within me as I praise God. I fully expect to speak with other tongues as You give me the utterance (Acts 2:4) In Jesus' Name Amen!

Begin to praise God for filling you with the Holy Spirit. Speak those words and syllables you receive—not in your own language, but the language given to you by the Holy Spirit. You have to use your own voice. God will not force you to speak. Don't be concerned with how it sounds. It is a heavenly language!

Continue with the blessing God has given you and pray in the spirit every day. You are born-again, and a Spirit-filled believer. You'll never be the same! Find a good church that boldly preaches God's Word and obeys it. Become part of a church family who will love and care for you as you love and care for them.

ABOUT THE AUTHOR

Norman Weber was born and raised in Windsor, Ontario, Canada. He attended high school and upon graduation joined a chartered accountant organization and apprenticed for five years and wrote exams each year. Upon the successful completion of this work, he received a CA degree. He worked in the industry for twenty years and twenty-two years in public accounting. He accepted Jesus as his Lord and Savior in 1971 and was filled with the Holy Spirit and was speaking in tongues in 1973. He was involved in leadership of several prayer meetings and became involved in a Christian ministry called Full Gospel Business Men's Fellowship. He eventually became a national director and was the national treasurer for nine years. He has spoken across Canada, in the United States, and in Australia. He has experienced the anointing of the Lord as he shares testimonies of what God has done in his life. He also moves in the gifts of the Holy Spirit. He resides with his wife in the rural area near Owen Sound, Ontario, and manages an apple orchard of 2,800 trees organically grown.

CPSIA information can be obtained
at www.ICGtesting.com
Printed in the USA
LVHW090738300619
622600LV00001BA/18/P

9 781640 798779